Agile Synergy Methodology

Critical Reflections on the Application of Agile Frameworks in Heterogeneous Teams

Stefano Galati

Copyright © 2024 Stefano Galati
All right reserved.
ISBN-13: 9798343969931
Independently published

Cover image:
Dietmar Rabich
(https://commons.wikimedia.org/wiki/File:Buntstifte_--_2021_--_9156.jpg), https://creativecommons.org/licenses/by-sa/4.0/legalcode

to Ilaria, my strength, my everything.

Prologue

In a rapidly changing world, where change is the only constant, the need for adaptability and flexibility in every aspect of business has become crucial. In this context, "Agile Synergy Methodology: Critical Reflections on the Application of Agile Frameworks in Heterogeneous Teams" emerges—not as a new methodology, but as a thoughtful and critical analysis of the challenges that agile methods encounter in modern organizations, especially when applied to heterogeneous teams.

In the pages that follow, you will not find a set of fixed rules or a new system for addressing change, but rather a reflection on the reality of agility today, across various business contexts. This book explores how existing agile principles can be tested in complex and diverse environments, and what the main challenges are in applying these frameworks to groups with differing skills, cultures, and objectives.

The book is dedicated to leaders, innovators, and all those on the front lines of facing the difficulties of change—those who confront the challenges of practical application of agile methodologies every day. It is aimed at those who, despite the challenges, are seeking better ways to work, collaborate, and grow in increasingly dynamic and diverse environments.

Through real case studies, practical examples, and critical reflections, I will guide you in analyzing the fundamental concepts of agile frameworks and their applications, highlighting the limits and opportunities these tools offer in heterogeneous teams. I do not offer definitive solutions, but rather an invitation to reflect, to question existing practices, and to open your mind to new possibilities for adapting agility to more complex business contexts.

"Agile Synergy Methodology" is not just a book to read; it is a starting point for broader reflection on agility and the challenges that the modern workplace imposes. Be prepared to explore the limits and potentials of what you already know as we together tackle the open questions surrounding the application of agile methods in a global and ever-evolving context.

Why read this book?

If you find yourself flipping through these pages, you likely share a fundamental question with many professionals around the world: how can we do better? In an era of rapid and often unpredictable changes, the answer to this question is essential not only for success but for the very survival of our organizations.

"Agile Synergy Methodology" is not a universal panacea, nor does it claim to be the only pathway to efficiency and innovation. However, it offers a fresh and holistic perspective on project management that might be just what you need. This book is for those who feel there must be a better way to do things, who are ready to challenge the conventional, and who are open to exploring new strategies to guide their teams toward success.

Through clear language, concrete examples, and a pragmatic structure, this book aims to guide you through the principles of Agile Synergy. It is an ideal read for both newcomers to agility and veterans seeking new perspectives. Here, you will discover how small changes in mindset and daily practices can lead to significant improvements in productivity, work quality, and team satisfaction.

Read this book if you are curious about how adaptability, collaboration, and continuous improvement can be seamlessly integrated into your project management. Whether you are a leader, a team member, or simply an enthusiast of organizational effectiveness, you will find insights and practical tools within these pages to embark on your journey toward a more agile and synergistic way of working.

Ultimately, read "Agile Synergy Methodology" not because it promises definitive answers, but because it equips you with the right questions and inspires you to find your solutions, tailored to your unique and ever-evolving context. Begin this journey with us and discover how to transform challenges into opportunities for growth and innovation.

Table of Contents

PROLOGUE... VI
WHY READ THIS BOOK? VII
TABLE OF CONTENTS X
THE GENESIS OF AGILE SYNERGY ANALYSIS 3
GUIDING PRICIPLES 4
ADAPTING AGILITY TO SPECIFIC CONTEXTS 6

Chapter 1 - Reflections on the Origins and Evolution of Agility

1.1 INTRODUCTION 13
1.2 THE ROOTS OF AGILITY 14
1.3 AGILITY TODAY: AN EVOLVING CONCEPT 17
1.4 CRITICAL REFLECTION ON AGILE FRAMEWORKS 20

Chapter 2 - A Fabric of Methodologies

2.1 INTRODUCTION 27
2.2 THE HYBRIDIZATION OF METHODOLOGIES 28
2.3 WHEN A FRAMEWORK IS NOT ENOUGH 31
2.4 HYBRIDIZATION AS A RESPONSE TO THE CHALLENGES OF HETEROGENEOUS TEAM.. 34
2.5 THE BENEFITS OF HYBRIDIZATION 38
2.6 CHALLENGES AND LIMITATIONS OF HYBRIDIZATION 42
2.7 CONCLUSION... 46

Chapter 3 – Clear Roles and Responsibilities

3.1 INTRODUCTION TO TRADITIONAL AGILE ROLES 51
3.2 THE ROLE OF THE SCRUM MASTER: FACILITATION AND INTERCULTURALITY 54
3.3 THE PRODUCT OWNER: BALANCING GLOBAL STAKEHOLDERS.......... 58

3.4 THE DEVELOPMENT TEAM: COLLABORATION AMONG DIVERSE DISCIPLINES AND SKILLS 62

3.5 ADAPTING ROLES TO TEAM NEEDS 67

3.6 COMMUNICATION IN TEAMS 72

3.7 CROSS-FUNCTIONAL SKILLS IN HETEROGENEOUS TEAMS 76

Chapter 4 – Integration of Methodologies

4.1 CHALLENGES OF INTEGRATING DIFFERENT AGILE FRAMEWORKS 85

4.2 THE IMPORTANCE OF CLEAR GUIDANCE 89

4.3 CASE STUDY: A MULTICULTURAL TECH STARTUP 93

4.4 ADAPTING FRAMEWORKS TO LOCAL AND GLOBAL NEEDS 95

4.5 REDUCING UNCERTAINTY THROUGH STANDARDIZATION 97

4.6 CONCLUSION 99

Chapter 5 – Evaluation of ROI in the Adoption of Agile Methodologies

5.1 ROI OF AGILITY: EXPECTED BENEFITS 105

5.2 CHALLENGES AND HIDDEN COSTS OF ADOPTING AGILITY IN HETEROGENEOUS TEAMS 107

5.3. WHEN AGILITY IS FORCED: NEGATIVE IMPACT ON ROI 109

5.4. MAXIMIZING ROI THROUGH AGILE ADAPTATION 111

5.5. CONCLUSION: A MORE INFORMED ROI 114

Chapter 6 – The Moments of Agility in Heterogeneous Teams - More than Events, a True Momentum

6.1 THE PLANNING MOMENT 121

6.2 THE ITERATIVE DEVELOPMENT MOMENT 125

6.3 THE CONTINUOUS FEEDBACK MOMENT 129

6.4 THE REVIEW AND IMPROVEMENT MOMENT 133

6.5 THE STAKEHOLDER ENGAGEMENT MOMENT 136

6.6. MOMENTUM OF AGILE EVENTS IN HETEROGENEOUS TEAMS - CONCLUSION 139

Chapter 7 - Change Management in Heterogeneous Teams

7.1 PREPARING THE TEAM FOR CHANGE 143

7.2. ACTIVE INVOLVEMENT OF ALL TEAM MEMBERS 146

7.3. OVERCOMING RESISTANCE TO CHANGE 149

7.4. ADAPTING CHANGE TO TEAMS DYNAMICS 152

7.5. MONITORING PROGRESS AND IMPACT OF CHANGE 156

7.6. STRENGTHENING TEAM COHESION DURING CHANGE................... 159

7.7. CONCLUSION OF THE CHAPTER: ADAPTING CHANGE TO HETEROGENEOUS TEAMS.. 163

Chapter 8 - Continuous Adaptation and Review in Heterogeneous Teams

8.1 STRATEGIC INCLUSION IN THE PRIORITIZATION DECISION-MAKING PROCESS 167

8.2. MANAGING PRIORITY CHANGES IN MULTIDISCIPLINARY TEAMS .. 170

8.3. CASE STUDY: R&D IN A LARGE MANUFACTURING COMPANY 173

8.4. ADAPTATION AND PRIORIZATION IN HETEROGENEOUS TEAMS 176

8.5. CONCLUSION OF THE CHAPTER: ADAPTATION AS A TOOL FOR SUCCESS IN HETEROGENEOUS TEAMS 179

Chapter 9 - The Value of Reflection and Continuous Improvement in Heterogeneous Teams

9.1. THE VALUE OF CONTINUOUS REFLECTION IN HETEROGENEOUS TEAMS 185

9.2. IMPLEMENTING CONTINUOUS IMPROVEMENT IN HETEROGENEOUS TEAMS 188

9.3. CASE STUDY: A TEAM OPERATING ACROSS MULTIPLE COUNTRIES WITH DIFFERENT REGULATORY.. 191

9.4. ADAPTATION AND PROACTIVITY IN HETEROGENEOUS TEAMS 195

Chapter 10 - Maintaining Strategic Vision in Heterogeneous Teams

10.1 THE STRATEGIC VISION IN AN AGILE ENVIRONMENT 201

10.2. BALANCING STRATEGIC VISION WITH OPERATIONAL AGILITY 205

10.3. MANAGING DIVERGENCES BETWEEN VISION AND OPERATIONS. 207

10.4. MAINTAINING CONSISTENCY IN VISION ACROSS DIVERSE TEAMS 209

10.5. PROMOTING AUTONOMY WHILE MAINTAINING ALIGNMENT WITH VISION 212

10.6. CONTINUOUS ADAPTATION TO THE STRATEGIC VISION 215

Chapter 11 - Collaboration and Innovation in Diverse Teams

11.1. CHALLENGES IN COLLABORATION AMONG DIVERSE TEAMS 221

11.2. STRATEGIES TO PROMOTE COLLABORATION IN DIVERSE TEAMS . 224

11.3. MANAGING COLLABORATION CHALLENGES IN DIVERSE TEAMS .. 228

11.4. FOSTERING CREATIVITY AND INNOVATION IN DIVERSE TEAMS ... 231

11.5. MANAGING CONFLICTS IN DIVERSE TEAMS 234

Chapter 12 - Performance Evaluation in Diverse Teams

12.1. EQUITY IN PERFORMANCE EVALUATION 241

12.2. MEASURING PERFORMANCE IN DIVERSE TEAMS 245

12.3. ADAPTING ASSESSMENTS TO TEAM DIVERSITY 248

12.4. MONITORING AND ADAPTING EVALUATION PARAMETERS 251

Chapter 13 - The Holistic Approach in IT: A Paradigm for Diverse Teams and Complex Projects

13.1. DEFINITION AND PRINCIPLES OF THE HOLISTIC APPROACH IN BUSINESS AGILITY 257

13.2. BENEFITS OF THE HOLISTIC APPROACH 259

13.3. CONCLUSION: EMBRACING HOLISM IN THE DIGITAL AGE 261

Chapter 14 - Proactive Change Management: Anticipating and Adapting in the Agile Era

14.1. MANAGING PAUSES AND RESUMING PROJECTS 267
14.2. ADAPTIVE PLANNING MODEL 269
14.3. RISK MANAGEMENT TOOLD AND CONTINGENCY PLANNING 271

Chapter 15 - Towards an Agile Future: Maturity, Limits, and Next Horizons

15.1. HOLISM AS A FOUNDATION FOR INNOVATION AND RESILIENCE . 279
15.2. INTEGRATING THE ORGANIZATIONAL DIMENSION AND GLOBAL STRATEGY 281
15.3. PREPARING FOR THE FUTURE: THE EVOLUTION OF AGILITY AND ITS LIMITS 284

REFERENCES.. 289

Introductory Section

Analyzing the strengths and limitations of agile methodologies in an increasingly complex business environment is more necessary now than ever. This book does not aim to propose a new method but rather to explore how established agile practices can be adapted and optimized to meet the increasingly diverse and complex needs of modern organizations.

"Agile Synergy" is not an alternative framework but a means to promote critical reflection on the limits and potential of agility in its current state. The goal is to investigate how these approaches can be reinterpreted and personalized to address complex and dynamic scenarios, without introducing new rules, but by fostering greater synergy among people, skills, and processes.

The Genesis of Agile Synergy Analysis

The starting point for this reflection is the realization that, despite the success of agile frameworks, many organizations struggle to translate them into effective solutions in real-world contexts. Existing methodologies, often seen as too rigid or generic, may not be sufficient to tackle the modern challenges of environments characterized by high technological, cultural, and operational diversity.

The objective of this book is to investigate the possibilities for adapting agility and its fundamental principles to better address the concrete needs of organizations. The key is not to create new rules but to understand how to collaborate effectively in interdisciplinary and dynamic contexts, valuing differences and promoting synergies among diverse skills and business processes.

Guiding Priciples

The reflection on how to adapt agility to complex business contexts is based on several key principles:

1. **Adaptability and Flexibility:** The ability to respond quickly to changes is crucial in rapidly evolving environments. Rather than seeking rigid solutions, the goal is to develop intrinsic flexibility that allows teams to evolve based on circumstances without being constrained by predefined patterns.
2. **Collaboration and Communication:** Synergy among teams and open communication are fundamental to success in complex environments. Fostering continuous dialogue and interdisciplinary collaboration enables better problem-solving and ongoing innovation.
3. **Continuous Innovation:** Agility is not just about managing change but leveraging it as a driver for constant improvement. The pursuit of innovative solutions

is at the heart of every iteration, ensuring that agile practices remain relevant and effective in the face of new challenges.

4. **Customization and Contextual Adaptation:** Organizations, projects, and teams are not all the same. This approach explores how existing methodologies can be tailored to specific contexts, respecting corporate culture and the skills of individual team members.

5. **Focus on Results:** True agility is measured not just by efficient processes but primarily by the ability to generate real and tangible value. The goal is not to follow a method for its own sake but to ensure that each iteration delivers concrete, measurable, and relevant results for the organization.

Through this analysis, we aim to explore how the principles of agility can be reinterpreted and personalized to better address modern challenges. The Agile Synergy approach thus becomes a tool for promoting critical and constructive reflection rather than a new methodology to be rigidly followed.

Adapting Agility to Specific Contexts

The approach explored in this book does not propose a new methodology but rather reflects on how agile principles and practices can be adapted to a multitude of professional contexts. Existing agile methodologies, while powerful, are not without their challenges. From tech startups to large multinationals, there are contexts that require a critical and mindful adaptation of agile principles.

• **Tech Startups:** In startups, agility can serve as a catalyst for rapid innovation, but it can sometimes be challenging to balance speed and quality. Analyzing how startups can maintain a high development pace without sacrificing product solidity is one of the key reflections.

• **Large Multinationals:** Agility in complex business contexts, with multiple departments and conflicting objectives, often encounters difficulties. The challenge is to find a balance between global consistency and local flexibility.

Continuous Evaluation and Contextual Adaptation

Rather than a rigid system, this book explores how continuous evaluation and contextual adaptation can become integral parts of agility. Regular moments of reflection within teams can represent opportunities to align with business goals, monitor progress, and make necessary adjustments without compromising operational flexibility.

•   **Evaluation Moments:** These serve as critical checkpoints where a team reflects on the results achieved, examines strategic alignment, and assesses the need for changes.
•   **Stakeholder Engagement:** Maintaining ongoing dialogue with stakeholders is crucial to balancing business needs with the operational capacity of the team.

Benefits and Limitations of Adopting Agile Practices

The adoption of agile practices, when well-adapted and contextualized, can lead to significant benefits, including increased flexibility and a greater capacity to respond to market needs. However, it is not without limitations. This book critically examines the aspects related to the ROI of agile practices, also considering the risks of application in non-ideal contexts.

•   **Increased Flexibility:** Organizations that adopt agile practices often enhance their ability to adapt to market changes. However, this can also pose the risk of losing focus on long-term objectives.
•   **Managing Uncertainty:** Agility improves uncertainty management, but in some contexts, the lack of rigid planning can generate inefficiencies and misunderstandings.

In summary, the analysis proposed in this book aims to explore how agile practices can be adapted and made more effective in diverse contexts, offering a tool for critical reflection and continuous improvement rather than the adoption of a new method.

This restructured approach emphasizes the critical analysis of existing agile practices and how they can be adapted while maintaining the idea of flexibility and ongoing reflection without introducing a new methodology.

SECTION 1: The Foundations

Chapter 1 – Reflections on the Origins and Evolution of Agility

Chapter 1
Reflections on the Origins and Evolution of Agility

Chapter 1 – Reflections on the Origins and Evolution of Agility

Chapter 1 – Reflections on the Origins and Evolution of Agility

1.1 Introduction

In the current context, characterized by rapid technological changes and increasingly competitive markets, the need for a flexible and dynamic approach to project management has become an essential priority. Agile methodologies, initially developed to address software development needs, have quickly spread to many other sectors, aiming to provide organizations with greater adaptability and responsiveness to change.

Among the most well-known agile methodologies are Scrum, Kanban, Extreme Programming (XP), and Crystal Clear/Yellow. Each of these practices has introduced significant innovations in project management. For instance, Scrum focuses on short iterative work cycles and a clear definition of roles within the team; Kanban offers a visual system for workflow management, emphasizing process optimization; XP highlights the importance of continuous feedback and technical excellence; while Crystal adopts a lighter, more adaptable approach, stressing the importance of communication within teams.

However, while each of these methodologies has proven effective in specific contexts, many organizations face challenges in applying a single framework to more complex and diverse realities. The need to integrate the strengths of different methodologies has become apparent, especially in heterogeneous teams operating in environments characterized by uncertainty and continuous change.

In this framework, there emerges a need for a more flexible and customizable approach. This is not about creating a new methodology but reflecting on how existing agile principles can be combined and adapted to tackle modern challenges. Adaptability, collaboration, and efficiency remain central, but with a greater emphasis on integrating frameworks and their constant refinement based on context.

This chapter will examine the roots of the most widely used agile methodologies and reflect on how they must evolve to meet today's challenges.

1.2 The Roots of Agility

Agility as a concept and organizational practice has deep roots that trace back to a crucial moment in the world of software development. In 2001, a group of industry experts convened to draft what would become the Agile Manifesto, a foundational document outlining the four values and twelve core principles upon which the agile movement is based. The primary goal was to address the increasing complexity and ineffectiveness of traditional project management methods, such as the waterfall model, which often proved too rigid for a rapidly evolving environment.

1.2.1 Scrum

Scrum is one of the first methodologies to emerge from the agile revolution. Created to address the need for rapid iterations and frequent feedback, Scrum introduces a structured development cycle centered around short sprints, with well-defined roles (Scrum Master, Product Owner, Development Team) and specific events such as the Daily Scrum and Sprint Retrospective. However, despite its success in software development teams, Scrum can be less effective in contexts where teams are distributed or operate in non-technical environments.

1.2.2 Kanban

Originally developed by Toyota for industrial production, Kanban has found new life in the agile world. This visual system for workflow management allows teams to optimize processes and continuously improve activity flow. While very flexible and applicable in a wide range of contexts, Kanban requires ongoing attention to workload management, which can be challenging in less structured teams or those unaccustomed to operational transparency.

1.2.3 Extreme Programming (XP)

Extreme Programming (XP), one of the earliest agile frameworks, focuses on improving software quality and the ability to respond to changes through a continuous and iterative development cycle. XP highlights collaboration between developers and clients, promoting practices such as pair programming, continuous testing, and frequent feedback. However, XP is heavily rooted in the context of software development, and although flexible, it can be difficult to adapt to teams operating in different sectors.

1.2.4 Crystal

Crystal, less known compared to Scrum or XP, is a lighter and more flexible framework. Created by Alistair Cockburn, Crystal emphasizes the adaptability of processes and communication within the team. This approach recognizes that every project is different and that there is no one-size-fits-all method. Crystal has proven effective in environments where direct communication and simplicity are essential, but in more complex or highly structured contexts, it can be challenging to maintain the necessary lightness.

1.2.5 The Challenge of Universal Application

Despite the successes and popularity of these methodologies, it is clear that none can be considered the definitive solution for every context. Each framework presents significant advantages in certain environments but also evident limitations when applied to more heterogeneous realities. Modern companies, especially those with diverse teams in terms of skills, geography, or culture, often find themselves needing to integrate different methodologies or deeply adapt them to achieve tangible results.

The evolution of agility therefore requires critical thinking: existing methodologies must be viewed not as rigid prescriptions but as starting points to be continuously adapted based on the specific context.

1.3 Agility Today: An Evolving Concept

Over the past twenty years, agility has undergone significant evolution, expanding far beyond the realm of software development. Today, agile methodologies have been adopted by companies across a wide range of sectors, including marketing, manufacturing, human resources, research and development, and many others. This broadening of agility has led to new challenges, especially when these practices are applied in contexts that differ radically from the technology sector in which they originated.

1.3.1 The Challenge of Complexity

With the expansion of agility into more complex business contexts, the need for adapting existing methodologies has become evident. Today's organizational structures are often characterized by geographically distributed teams with heterogeneous skills and diverse work cultures. In these situations, applying a traditional agile framework like Scrum or Kanban may prove ineffective without significant customization.

For example, in global companies operating in regulated markets, agile methodologies must often coexist with compliance requirements and regulatory constraints. This reality introduces a level of complexity that was not anticipated by the creators of the original agile methodologies. Thus, the capacity for adaptation and flexibility, which is one of the core principles of agility, becomes not just desirable but essential.

1.3.2 Diversification of Agile Applications

Agility has demonstrated its usefulness in various sectors, but with specific adaptations. For instance:

• Marketing: Here, agility is used to create flexible and responsive campaigns that can quickly adapt to market feedback and changing trends. However, the traditional Scrum approach can be challenging to apply, as feedback cycles in marketing are often longer than those typical in software development.

• Manufacturing: In this context, methodologies like Kanban have found excellent application, especially in lean manufacturing lines. However, the high standardization required in these environments limits the capacity for experimentation and rapid adaptation, two pillars of agility.

• Human Resources: Agility has also begun to transform people management. Processes such as recruiting, skill development, and performance management are adopting agile practices to improve flexibility and adaptability.

1.3.3 The Need for a Hybrid Approach

With the increasing diversity in application contexts, it has become clear that no single agile framework is sufficient to meet all the needs of a modern organization. Companies that have been most successful in adopting agile practices are those that have managed to combine elements from different methodologies, tailoring them to their specific needs. This hybrid approach allows for balancing the flexibility needed to navigate changes with the structure essential for maintaining consistency and strategic direction.

For instance, many companies choose to use Scrum for project lifecycle management, Kanban for managing daily workflow, and XP to ensure product quality through continuous development practices. This type of hybrid approach allows for the integration of the strengths of each framework and their flexible application, depending on the needs of the team or project.

1.3.4 Adaptive Agility

Today, agility must be viewed as a continuously evolving concept. The practices and principles that worked ten years ago may no longer be suitable for today's business contexts, and methodologies must be constantly revisited. This does not mean that agility has become obsolete; rather, its applications must be more contextual and less dogmatic.

The future of agility lies not in adopting a single rigid framework but in the ability to combine and adapt agile practices according to needs. Companies that can manage this flexibility will be those that can derive the greatest long-term benefits from agility.

1.4 Critical Reflection on Agile Frameworks

In recent years, many organizations have embarked on adopting agile methodologies such as Scrum, Kanban, XP, and Crystal, with the expectation of improving efficiency and flexibility. However, despite the successes reported in various sectors, it has become clear that the application of these frameworks is not without limitations. The nature of today's teams and organizations—often distributed, interdisciplinary, and culturally heterogeneous—has highlighted some weaknesses of traditional agile models, necessitating a rethinking of how and where these tools can be effectively utilized.

1.4.1 Scrum: Rigid in Dynamic Environments?

Scrum was one of the first agile frameworks to achieve widespread adoption, particularly in technology organizations. However, over time, it has become evident that its rigid structure, with well-defined roles and mandatory events, can conflict with business contexts that require greater flexibility or operate in less technical environments. For example, in creative teams or in long-term projects with less predictable work cycles, the strict application of Scrum can prove more of an obstacle than an advantage.

Case Study: A Multicultural Tech Startup

A multicultural team, distributed across three continents, attempted to adopt Scrum to manage the development of a new product. Despite initial progress, issues related to time zone synchronization and cultural barriers made daily events like the Daily Scrum challenging. The need to frequently modify plans and sprints due to market demands further highlighted the framework's lack of flexibility. This led the team to reduce the number of formal events and adopt Kanban practices to better manage workflow, making the process smoother and more suited to their context.

1.4.2 Kanban: Limitations in Teamwork

Kanban offers a flexible approach to managing work, focusing on the continuous flow of tasks and visualizing ongoing work. However, one of Kanban's main limitations is that it can overlook the relational aspects of teamwork. While Scrum imposes a certain level of interaction among team members, Kanban focuses more on process optimization. This can lead to a lack of cohesion within the team, especially in contexts where collaboration is essential.

Case Study: An R&D Team in a Large Manufacturing Company

A large research and development team in a multinational attempted to adopt Kanban to improve workflow management and reduce delivery times. Although Kanban resulted in greater transparency and more effective task management, the team began to experience a lack of internal cohesion. The absence of structured moments to reflect and improve as a group led to fragmentation, with team members working increasingly in isolation. The solution was to integrate elements of Scrum, such as retrospectives, to restore interaction among team members and enhance collaboration.

1.4.3 XP: Effective Only for Technical Teams?

Extreme Programming (XP) is a methodology that focuses on technical excellence and collaboration between developers and clients. However, it is heavily rooted in the software development context. In non-technical teams or environments where code quality is not the primary objective, XP can be challenging to apply, and its emphasis on continuous feedback may be less relevant.

1.4.4 Crystal: An Approach That Is Too Light?

Crystal, with its emphasis on simplicity and direct communication, is ideal for small teams and less complex projects. However, in more structured and regulated environments where more formal procedures are required, Crystal can prove too lightweight, lacking the robustness needed to manage large-scale projects or those with a strong quality control component.

1.4.5 Integrating Different Methodologies: Towards a Hybrid Approach

Given the complex and diverse nature of modern organizations, a hybrid approach is often the most effective solution. Many teams find that combining elements from different agile frameworks allows them to better address the challenges of their specific context. This approach not only capitalizes on the strengths of each method but also avoids the limitations inherent in the rigid application of a single framework.

1.4.6 Conclusion

Traditional agile methodologies have proven effective in many contexts, but today's work environment, characterized by heterogeneous and distributed teams, requires a more flexible and adaptive approach. No agile framework can be considered a universal solution, and the future of agility lies in organizations' ability to customize and combine agile practices according to their specific needs.

Chapter 1 – Reflections on the Origins and Evolution of Agility

Chapter 2

A Fabric of Methodologies

Chapter 2 – A Fabric of Methodologies

2.1 Introduction

In the realm of agile project management, no single framework can meet all business needs, especially when it comes to addressing the complexity of heterogeneous teams that are geographically distributed or possess multidisciplinary skills. Agile methodologies such as Scrum, Kanban, and Extreme Programming (XP), while extremely effective in certain contexts, have limitations when applied rigidly to organizations with diverse requirements.

Companies operating in complex environments, characterized by rapid change and the need for flexibility, increasingly adopt a hybrid approach, combining elements from various agile methodologies to create a customized solution. This type of hybridization allows organizations to leverage the strengths of each framework and adapt them to the specificities of the project, enhancing their ability to respond quickly to changes without sacrificing efficiency or structure.

Far from being a standalone new methodology, the hybridization of agile practices is a natural response to the needs of modern businesses. In this chapter, we will explore how the combination of agile methodologies has become an increasingly common practice to address the specific challenges that heterogeneous teams encounter in their projects.

2.2 The Hybridization of Methodologies

The hybridization of agile methodologies represents the practice of combining elements from different frameworks to more effectively address the unique challenges presented by each project and organization. This approach has proven particularly useful for companies operating in complex and diverse contexts, where the rigid adoption of a single framework may be insufficient. Hybridization allows organizations to leverage the strengths of multiple methodologies, adapting them to the specific needs of the project, team, or organizational environment.

Companies that adopt hybridization do so to create a more flexible and personalized approach. A typical example is the integration of Scrum and Kanban, two agile methodologies that complement each other. Scrum focuses on iterative work management through well-defined cycles called sprints, which help establish clear and measurable short-term objectives. This approach is beneficial for teams working on projects that require regular releases of product increments. However, some teams find that Scrum alone is not sufficient to manage the continuous flow of daily activities, especially in contexts where new priorities or unforeseen changes frequently arise.

In these cases, Kanban can be integrated to enhance workflow management, allowing teams to visualize ongoing activities, track progress, and identify bottlenecks in the process. Kanban, with its visual and continuous approach, helps improve transparency and communication, providing a clear overview of all ongoing work, regardless of the development cycle. The integration of the two approaches thus balances Scrum's structured iteration with Kanban's operational flexibility, creating a more agile and responsive system.

Another example of hybridization is the use of practices from Extreme Programming (XP) to ensure technical quality in software development projects. XP emphasizes practices such as pair programming, continuous integration, and automated testing—all activities that contribute to reducing defects and improving code quality. When combined with Scrum or Kanban, XP provides the technical discipline necessary to ensure that the final product is not only developed quickly but also technically sound.

Hybridization is not limited to technological contexts. Organizations operating in non-technical sectors are also adopting hybrid agile approaches to enhance their ability to respond quickly to market changes. A common example is the integration of agile practices with traditional project management processes. In companies with strict governance requirements, such as those in regulated industries (e.g., finance or healthcare), agility must coexist with the need to follow formal protocols and rigorous documentation. In this context, the hybridization of methodologies allows for the combination of the flexibility and speed of agile practices with the necessary regulatory compliance, ensuring that projects remain aligned with market and regulatory expectations.

The hybridization of methodologies becomes particularly important when an organization is managing heterogeneous teams. Geographically distributed teams or those composed of members with interdisciplinary skills can greatly benefit from a combination of frameworks. In these cases, practices like Scrum can promote collaboration and work synchronization through events like sprint reviews and daily stand-ups, while Kanban can be used to track continuous workflow, monitor real-time progress, and manage bottlenecks.

In an organization working on complex projects, the ability to adapt and combine agile methodologies is essential for maintaining a high level of efficiency and responding swiftly to changes. This hybridization also improves scalability, allowing companies to apply agile practices on a large scale while maintaining the flexibility necessary to manage smaller teams with specific needs. The hybrid approach not only increases organizational flexibility but also enhances communication among teams, encouraging the adoption of agile practices tailored to the specific context.

In summary, the hybridization of agile methodologies has become a necessity for modern companies facing complex and dynamic work environments. This approach allows organizations to draw on the best features of various frameworks, avoiding the limitations inherent in the rigid application of a single methodology.

2.3 When a Framework Is Not Enough

Despite the demonstrated effectiveness of agile methodologies such as Scrum, Kanban, and XP, there are contexts and situations where the application of a single framework is insufficient to address the complexities of a project. Limitations particularly arise when teams operate in diverse contexts, such as geographically distributed teams, interdisciplinary projects, or highly regulated sectors, where needs and expectations vary considerably.

2.3.1 Scrum: Limitations of a Rigid Framework

Scrum is distinguished by its rigid structure and well-defined events, such as sprint planning, daily stand-ups, and sprint retrospectives. However, this structure can become problematic in environments where priorities change rapidly or where work does not lend itself to a clear division into predetermined sprint durations. For example, a team working in a research and development sector might find it challenging to adhere to two- or four-week cycles, as task completion times can be highly variable and dependent on numerous external factors.

Another example of Scrum's limitation emerges in geographically distributed teams, where differing time zones make participation in daily events like the stand-up difficult. The rigidity of the framework can lead to misalignments within the team, especially if there is no opportunity to adapt events to the specific needs of the group. In these situations, the rigid application of Scrum can create inefficiencies and frustrations among team members, resulting in outcomes that fall short of expectations.

2.3.2 Kanban: Excessive Flexibility

On the other hand, Kanban offers an extremely flexible approach, allowing teams to manage workflow continuously without the need to divide work into defined cycles. However, this flexibility can also be a limitation. In projects requiring stricter planning or where clear deadlines are essential, Kanban may prove insufficient. The absence of sprints or predetermined work cycles can make it challenging to manage stakeholder expectations, who may require greater predictability regarding completion times and interim results.

Additionally, in less mature teams or those with less experience in self-organization, Kanban can lead to a lack of cohesion and collaboration, as team members focus more on their individual activities rather than the overall work of the group. Without the structured events of Scrum, it can be difficult to maintain an overview of the project and ensure that everyone is aligned on the goals to be achieved.

2.3.3 XP: Technical Limits in Non-Software Contexts

Extreme Programming (XP) is a highly regarded methodology for software development projects, thanks to its focus on technical excellence and continuous iteration. However, XP proves less applicable in non-technical contexts or in teams that do not require specific technical practices such as pair programming or continuous integration. In projects that do not involve software development, XP may seem overly focused on technical aspects, losing sight of the importance of overall project management and collaboration among team members.

Even in software projects, XP can be too focused on technical quality and lack a long-term strategic focus. This can lead to situations where the team becomes overly absorbed in technical details at the expense of the overall project vision, risking the loss of sight of business objectives or stakeholder needs.

2.3.4 Crystal: Too Light in Complex Contexts

Crystal, with its emphasis on lightness and process customization, is ideal for small teams and less complex projects. However, in more structured contexts or large-scale projects, Crystal may lack the robustness needed to manage operational complexity. Organizations operating in highly regulated sectors, where formal protocols and rigorous documentation are required, may find Crystal too lightweight to meet compliance and control needs.

Moreover, the lack of rigid rules and formal structures in Crystal can create confusion in larger or less experienced teams, which may require clearer guidance to manage workflow and ensure timely delivery of results.

2.3.5 When Hybridization Is the Solution

These examples highlight that no single agile methodology can perfectly address the needs of all organizational contexts. The limitations of each framework become more evident in projects that require continuous adaptation to new needs, stakeholder expectation management, or collaboration among heterogeneous and distributed teams. In these cases, hybridization of multiple methodologies emerges as the most natural and advantageous solution.

The integration of diverse practices allows teams to overcome the limitations of each framework by combining Kanban's adaptability with Scrum's structure or integrating XP's technical practices with the workflow management features offered by other frameworks. Adopting a hybrid approach enables teams to leverage the strengths of each methodology, effectively addressing the specific challenges of the project and improving overall performance.

In conclusion, when a single framework is not enough, hybridization provides the opportunity to create a tailored agile methodology to meet the needs of each project and organization, ensuring the flexibility and efficiency necessary to achieve objectives.

2.4 Hybridization as a Response to the Challenges of Heterogeneous Team

The adoption of agile methodologies is particularly challenging when it comes to managing heterogeneous teams. Diversity within a team can be a valuable asset, but it can also be a significant source of complexity. Heterogeneous teams may be characterized by geographical distribution, interdisciplinary skills, cultural and linguistic differences, and varying work styles. In these contexts, a rigid approach to a single agile methodology risks being ineffective, while a hybrid approach allows for balancing and harmonizing these diversities.

2.4.1 Managing Geographical Diversity

When team members are distributed across different time zones or locations, managing daily interactions and synchronizing work becomes a primary challenge. In a traditional agile context, such as Scrum, events like the daily stand-up or sprint planning require all team members to be present at the same time. However, this practice can become difficult, if not impossible, to maintain in distributed teams.

The hybridization of agile methodologies allows for overcoming this challenge by combining elements of Scrum and Kanban. For instance, the use of Kanban can improve workflow management and enable the team to handle activities more asynchronously, monitoring progress through a visual system like a Kanban board that shows the status of tasks regardless of team members' physical locations. At the same time, Scrum events can be maintained in a reduced format or on a weekly basis, ensuring there is a regular alignment moment without requiring daily synchronization.

2.4.2 Integrating Interdisciplinary Skills

Another complexity in heterogeneous teams concerns the management of diverse skills. In complex projects, it is common for teams to consist of members with very different professional backgrounds, such as engineers, designers, marketers, and product specialists. Each of these professional roles may have different needs, languages, and working styles, which can conflict if managed with a single agile approach.

To facilitate collaboration among diverse skills, hybridizing methodologies allows for adopting tools that better fit the various needs of the team. For example, Scrum can be used to manage the development cycle in short, well-defined iterations, while Design Thinking or elements of Lean Startup can be integrated to allow designers and product specialists to explore innovative solutions in less structured and more creative phases. This approach enables the alignment of technical work with creative endeavors, ensuring that interdisciplinarity does not become a hindrance but rather a competitive advantage.

2.4.3 Overcoming Cultural and Linguistic Barriers

In global or multicultural teams, linguistic and cultural differences can complicate collaboration. For example, some team members may come from contexts where hierarchy and formal decisions are highly valued, while others may prefer a more informal and collaborative approach. The rigid adoption of a single agile framework, such as Scrum, risks exacerbating these cultural differences, especially during decision-making phases or feedback sessions.

The hybridization of methodologies allows for customizing agile practices to better address the cultural sensitivities of the team. For instance, the structured aspects of Scrum can be maintained to ensure a clear definition of roles and responsibilities, while integrating Kanban elements to provide greater flexibility in work organization.

Additionally, the use of asynchronous collaboration tools, such as digital platforms for task management and communication, can reduce reliance on face-to-face meetings, which may be challenging to manage in multicultural teams with differing communication expectations.

2.4.4 The Importance of Continuous Communication and Alignment

In heterogeneous teams, maintaining clear and regular communication is essential to prevent differences from leading to misunderstandings or misalignments. A hybrid approach allows for using various tools to manage internal communication, such as the structured events of Scrum (e.g., sprint reviews or retrospectives) and continuous feedback practices from Extreme Programming (XP). These tools enable the team to continuously assess progress, quickly identify problems or inefficiencies, and correct the course without compromising work quality or collaboration among members.

In this context, hybridization facilitates the creation of a system where communication and continuous alignment among team members are ensured while maintaining the flexibility needed to adapt to various internal needs and dynamics.

2.4.5 Conclusion: Hybridization as a Tool for Cohesion in Heterogeneous Teams

The hybridization of agile methodologies is an effective response to the challenges that arise in heterogeneous teams. The integration of practices from different frameworks allows for better management of geographical, cultural, and disciplinary diversity within a team, ensuring operational flexibility without sacrificing structure and clarity. In this way, hybridization becomes not only a practical solution but a true tool for cohesion and harmonization, enabling teams to work together effectively despite their differences.

2.5 The Benefits of Hybridization

The hybridization of agile methodologies offers a wide range of benefits, especially in complex and dynamic contexts where a single framework cannot meet the needs of all stakeholders involved. Combining elements from multiple methodologies enables organizations to maintain flexibility and adaptability without losing sight of efficiency and quality. Below are the main benefits that hybridizing agile methodologies can offer.

2.5.1 Operational Flexibility

One of the most evident advantages of hybridization is the flexibility it provides to teams. The ability to draw on practices from various methodologies allows the project management process to be tailored to specific needs, rather than forcing the team to follow a single methodology that may not always be suitable. For example, a team might use Scrum to maintain iterative project management while introducing Kanban elements to monitor daily workflow and manage priorities dynamically.

This level of flexibility is particularly beneficial in projects where priorities or conditions change frequently, allowing teams to respond quickly to changes without compromising productivity or effectiveness. Furthermore, the flexibility of hybridization also enables methodologies to be adapted to the preferences and skills of team members, facilitating better integration and a more collaborative approach.

2.5.2 Scalability

The hybridization of agile methodologies provides an approach that can easily scale, both at the team and organizational levels. In a business context, a hybrid approach allows for adapting agile processes to teams of different sizes or functions while maintaining consistency in core principles and practices.

For instance, a large organization might use SAFe (Scaled Agile Framework) as an overarching structure to manage projects at the enterprise level while combining elements of Scrum and Kanban in smaller, focused development teams, maintaining an agile and iterative workflow. This hybrid approach enables organizations to grow without losing agility, maintaining the flexibility needed to respond to the demands of a constantly evolving market.

2.5.3 Quick Response to Changes

Another key advantage of hybridization is the ability to respond quickly and effectively to changes, both within the team and in the business or market context. In a dynamic environment, where priorities can change unpredictably, combining multiple methodologies allows teams to adapt rapidly without completely rethinking their work processes.

For example, a team using Scrum to manage iterative development can integrate Lean Startup principles to quickly experiment with new ideas and validate business hypotheses. This enables the team to respond more effectively to changes in the market or customer requirements without compromising the iterative structure provided by Scrum.

2.5.4 Improved Collaboration and Communication

A hybrid approach enhances collaboration among team members and communication between various stakeholders. Combining different methodologies allows for creating specific moments for structured communication and others for spontaneous collaboration. For instance, the transparency of Kanban, which visualizes the workflow in real-time, can be integrated with Scrum's structured retrospectives, fostering not only constant alignment but also continuous reflection and improvement of team dynamics.

Moreover, in business contexts where multiple interdisciplinary or distributed teams collaborate, hybridization allows for customizing communication practices to better fit the specific needs of the project or team, thereby improving interaction efficiency and reducing misunderstandings.

2.5.5 Enhanced Quality and Productivity

Hybridization not only enables greater flexibility but also improves the quality of work and productivity. By combining elements from Extreme Programming (XP), such as pair programming and test-driven development, with management practices like Scrum or Kanban, teams can ensure that work is not only delivered quickly but also of high quality.

For instance, a team using XP to maintain high coding standards can integrate Scrum's iterative approach to deliver product increments consistently and measurably. This allows for maintaining excellent technical quality without compromising delivery times, thereby improving overall project outcomes.

2.5.6 Adapting to the Needs of Heterogeneous Teams

As discussed previously, heterogeneous teams require a flexible approach that considers different skills, work styles, and geographical locations. Hybridization allows for customizing practices to better fit the specific needs of each team. For example, a distributed team might benefit from a combination of structured Scrum events and a more flexible workflow managed through Kanban.

This adaptability enables the harmonization of various work styles, ensuring that every team member can contribute effectively, regardless of differences in background or technical skills.

2.5.7 Conclusion: The Benefits of Hybridization

The hybridization of agile methodologies offers numerous advantages to modern organizations facing complex and dynamic challenges. The combination of flexibility, scalability, responsiveness to changes, improved collaboration and communication, along with increased quality and productivity, makes hybridization a powerful solution for enhancing the overall effectiveness of projects.

In an increasingly complex world, where teams must quickly adapt to new challenges, the hybridization of agile methodologies allows organizations to create a tailored approach that ensures the achievement of goals and continuous improvement.

2.6 Challenges and Limitations of Hybridization

Despite the numerous benefits offered by the hybridization of agile methodologies, this approach also presents certain challenges and limitations that organizations must carefully consider. Combining multiple agile frameworks can generate confusion, overlap in practices, and, if not managed properly, can lead to inefficiencies and difficulties in team alignment. Below, we explore some of the main challenges associated with hybridization and how to address them.

2.6.1 Management Complexity

Hybridization of methodologies can introduce a level of management complexity that goes well beyond what one might encounter when adopting a single framework. Integrating different practices requires a clear understanding of how each methodology operates and its interactions with other adopted approaches. If not managed correctly, the risk is to create confusion among team members, with overlapping or contradictory practices leading to inefficiencies.

For instance, a team attempting to combine Scrum and Kanban might find itself managing both rigid sprints and continuous workflow simultaneously, without a clear distinction of when to apply one or the other. This can result in poor work organization, risking team members becoming overwhelmed or losing sight of priorities. To avoid this situation, it is essential to establish clear governance and rules on how and when to use the different practices.

2.6.2 Alignment and Communication

In a hybridization context, maintaining constant alignment among team members can become more difficult. The introduction of different methodologies may create divisions within the team, especially if some members are more familiar or comfortable with one framework than others. The lack of effective communication can amplify this issue, leading to disconnections and misunderstandings that slow project progress.

A common example is the simultaneous adoption of Scrum and XP practices. If the technical team focuses on continuous improvement through XP practices like test-driven development, but other team members are not well-informed about XP principles, they may not fully understand why certain technical decisions are made. This misalignment can lead to frustrations and conflicts within the team.

To avoid these issues, it is crucial to establish clear communication channels and regular alignment practices, such as retrospectives and internal review moments. This allows all team members to have a common understanding of the methodologies in use and how they integrate into the project's context.

2.6.3 Difficulty in Maintaining Consistency

One of the main goals of agility is to ensure that the team maintains a clear direction and consistency in the processes and practices adopted. However, when combining multiple methodologies, the risk of losing consistency increases. Without clear guidance and defined rules on which practices to adopt at specific times, hybridization could lead to an inconsistent approach with unpredictable outcomes.

For example, if a team uses Scrum for its planning events and Kanban for managing workflow, there may be confusion about how to prioritize activities. This can lead to a disconnect between strategic planning and operational management, risking that project objectives are not met. To avoid these inconsistencies, it is important to establish clear integration between the methodologies, defining precise rules for managing transitions between frameworks.

2.6.4 Team Training and Skillsets

The hybridization of agile methodologies requires team members to have a solid understanding of the practices in use and to be able to effectively adopt different tools and processes. Training the team on various methodologies and ensuring comprehension can be challenging, especially in business contexts with high turnover or where team members have varying levels of experience.

If some team members are more experienced in one methodology than others, imbalances may emerge that slow progress and create barriers to collaboration. To address this challenge, it is important to invest in continuous training, providing team members with opportunities to learn new skills and gain a deep understanding of the principles of the agile methodologies adopted. Workshops, coaching, and mentoring sessions can be effective tools to help the team master the hybridization of practices.

2.6.5 Risk of Excessive Complexity

One of the main risks of hybridization is creating a system that is too complex and difficult to manage. Adding practices from different methodologies without a clear and structured approach can lead to excessive complexity, with redundant or unnecessary processes and events that slow down workflow instead of accelerating it.

For instance, a team trying to combine Scrum, Kanban, and XP might find itself overwhelmed by too many meetings, with retrospectives, planning sessions, and synchronizations accumulating and becoming unmanageable. The proliferation of events and processes can lead to team paralysis, reducing the capacity to make quick and efficient decisions.

To avoid this risk, it is essential to maintain a lean and focused approach. Hybridization should serve to improve processes, not to complicate them. The goal is to select only those practices that add real value to the team, eliminating those that are superfluous or redundant.

2.6.6 Conclusion: Managing Challenges and Limitations

Despite the challenges and limitations associated with the hybridization of agile methodologies, these can be managed with a structured and well-planned approach. It is essential for organizations to commit to maintaining clear process governance, providing adequate training for the team, and establishing clear communication and alignment rules. Hybridization should be seen as a process of continuous improvement, where practices are adapted and refined based on the specific needs of the project and the team.

With the right attention and care, the hybridization of agile methodologies can be a powerful tool for increasing team effectiveness, tackling complex projects, and enhancing the ability to respond to market changes.

2.7 Conclusion

The hybridization of agile methodologies is increasingly emerging as an effective response to the growing complexity of projects and teams in today's business world. We have seen how the combination of practices from various frameworks, such as Scrum, Kanban, Extreme Programming (XP), and others, offers a flexibility and adaptability that individual frameworks, taken in isolation, cannot guarantee.

In contexts characterized by rapid changes, shifting priorities, and the need to collaborate with heterogeneous and geographically distributed teams, hybridization allows organizations to optimize their workflow. The great advantage of this approach lies in its customization: it enables teams to choose the practices that best fit their specific needs, dynamically and consciously integrating various methodologies.

2.7.1. Critical Reflections on Hybridization

However, as discussed, hybridization is not without challenges. Managing complexity, maintaining alignment among team members, and the risk of overloading the process with too many practices are issues that must be addressed carefully. It is essential that hybridization does not become a disorganized accumulation of practices but is guided by clear logic and a constant focus on the project's objectives and the team's needs.

Organizations that adopt a hybrid approach must invest time and resources in continuous training, communication, and governance. Only in this way can they fully leverage the benefits of a hybrid approach without falling into its potential pitfalls.

2.7.2. Towards Continuous Change Management

A fundamental point that emerges from the analysis of hybridization is its ability to promote continuous change. In an environment where change is the only constant, the ability to adapt quickly to new conditions becomes a key competitive factor. The hybridization of agile methodologies not only supports this ability but encourages it, enabling teams to evolve and continually improve their processes in line with market challenges.

2.7.3. Hybridization as a Growth Tool

Ultimately, what hybridization represents is a tool for growth. It is not a rigid system to be applied mechanically but a dynamic approach that requires reflection, adaptation, and continuous learning. Hybridization allows teams to evolve as project needs and working conditions change, offering the flexibility necessary to thrive in an increasingly uncertain and competitive world.

In conclusion, the hybridization of agile methodologies represents one of the most promising paths for organizations looking to optimize their processes and improve operational effectiveness. The key to its success lies in balance: knowing which practices to adopt, how to integrate them, and, above all, when to adapt them to the specific needs of the project. Companies that can manage this balance will benefit not only from greater efficiency but also from an enhanced capacity to innovate, collaborate, and respond swiftly to future challenges.

If managed carefully, hybridization is not just a tactical strategy to improve processes but a strategic approach to prepare organizations for continuous change and sustainable growth.

Chapter 3
Clear Roles and Responsibilities

Chapter 3 – Clear Roles and Responsibilities

3.1 Introduction to Traditional Agile Roles

Traditional agile roles have been designed to facilitate the efficient functioning of teams and promote collaboration through clear structures. The three main roles in the Scrum framework—Scrum Master, Product Owner, and Development Team—each perform a specific function within the agile process.

• Scrum Master: The Scrum Master is the facilitator of the team. Their job is to ensure that agile practices are followed correctly, remove obstacles, and help the team work efficiently, shielding the group from external distractions. Their role is not that of a traditional manager but rather a facilitator who supports the team in achieving the goals set for the sprint.

• Product Owner: The Product Owner represents the voice of the customer within the team. They are responsible for managing and prioritizing the product backlog, ensuring that the team works on tasks that maximize value for the end user. The Product Owner acts as an intermediary between the development team and external stakeholders, translating market and customer needs into technical and functional specifications that the team can implement.

• Development Team: The Development Team consists of professionals who carry out the necessary activities to transform ideas into a functioning product. Traditionally, the development team is made up of professionals with specific technical skills (developers, designers, testers) who work together to deliver product increments at the end of each sprint. The team is characterized by a high level of self-organization, deciding how to achieve the objectives set by the Product Owner and collaborating closely to meet deadlines.

These roles were conceived for traditional agile teams, often homogeneous in terms of skills and located in the same physical space. The well-defined structure of roles and responsibilities facilitates collaboration and promotes an iterative and incremental process, where each team member knows exactly their task and how it fits into the overall project context.

However, as agility has expanded to sectors beyond software and has started being applied to heterogeneous teams, these roles have encountered new challenges. Modern teams are often geographically distributed and composed of individuals with interdisciplinary skills and cultural backgrounds. This context has necessitated an evolution of the concepts of Scrum Master, Product Owner, and Development Team, which can no longer be confined to their original tasks but must adapt to the new team dynamics.

3.1.1 New Challenges in Heterogeneous Teams

When teams become more diverse and distributed, traditional agile roles face complex issues:

- **Time Zones:** In globally distributed teams, coordinating daily meetings and synchronizations, such as the Daily Scrum, can be challenging. Traditional Scrum events may need to be adapted or even eliminated to allow teams to collaborate without requiring members to be synchronized at the same time.

• Interdisciplinary Skills: Modern teams often include not only developers but also designers, marketing experts, and other non-technical specialists. The Scrum Master must adapt practices to facilitate collaboration among professionals with very different skills and perspectives.

• Cultural Differences: In international teams, expectations about how to communicate, resolve issues, and make decisions can vary greatly. The Product Owner must navigate these cultural differences to ensure that all voices are heard and that decisions made reflect a global consensus.

3.1.2 The Evolution of Agile Roles

To respond to these challenges, traditional agile roles must evolve. The Scrum Master must also become an intercultural mediator and a facilitator of virtual communication, while the Product Owner must be able to balance multiple priorities from stakeholders scattered around the world. The Development Team must also adapt, learning to work more autonomously and self-organized, managing effective communication despite distance and professional differences.

This evolution requires that each traditional role retains its core tasks but expands to fit the complex reality of modern teams. The key to success lies in the ability to adapt and integrate new skills and approaches that facilitate collaboration and work in heterogeneous contexts.

In summary, while traditional agile roles remain fundamental, their application in modern teams requires flexibility and adaptation. The Scrum Master, Product Owner, and Development Team must evolve to manage the complexities of heterogeneous teams, integrating new skills and approaches to ensure the continuity of the agile process and the success of the project.

3.2 The Role of the Scrum Master: Facilitation and Interculturality

The Scrum Master, in its traditional definition, is the facilitator of the team and the guardian of the agile process. Their primary task is to ensure that the team correctly follows Scrum practices, that meetings are effective, that impediments are removed, and that the team can focus on value-added activities. The Scrum Master does not have a command role but acts as a "servant leader," supporting the team in achieving the goals set for the sprint.

However, in heterogeneous and distributed contexts, the role of the Scrum Master must expand and adapt to new challenges. With the rise of teams operating in different countries, with diverse cultures and across multiple time zones, the Scrum Master is not only a facilitator of the process but also needs to be a cultural mediator and an expert in managing remote communication. Under these conditions, the Scrum Master faces issues that go beyond merely removing technical or operational impediments.

3.2.1 Facilitation in Distributed Teams

In distributed teams, where members may work in different locations and time zones, the Scrum Master must be flexible in managing meetings and traditional events. Meetings like the Daily Scrum, which in a traditional context occur physically or virtually at the same time every day, can be difficult to manage when team members are spread across incompatible time zones. The Scrum Master must find ways to maintain open communication without overburdening team members with synchronized meetings that may not fit their schedules.

In some cases, the Daily Scrum may be replaced with asynchronous updates using tools like Slack, Jira, Confluence, or other collaborative platforms. The Scrum Master is responsible for ensuring that such updates are regular, clear, and easily accessible to the entire team. They must also monitor any communication issues that may arise from the lack of face-to-face interactions, ensuring that team members remain aligned on objectives and priorities.

3.2.2 Cultural Mediation

Another crucial challenge that the Scrum Master faces in a heterogeneous team is managing cultural differences. Team members from diverse cultural backgrounds may have different expectations regarding how work should be managed, how to communicate, and how decisions should be made. In some cultures, for example, a more hierarchical approach to task management may be preferred, while in others, autonomy and collective discussion are valued more.

The Scrum Master must be aware of these differences and take on the role of a mediator, facilitating communication and mutual understanding among team members. This requires intercultural sensitivity and the ability to adapt the facilitation style to meet the needs of each team member. For instance, the Scrum Master may need to balance more direct communication styles with those that are more implicit, creating a work environment where everyone feels comfortable contributing.

3.2.3 Managing Impediments in Complex Contexts

Within a heterogeneous team, the Scrum Master addresses not only traditional impediments (such as technical issues, operational blocks, or resource shortages) but also obstacles related to the complexity of interactions among team members. For example, time zone differences, language barriers, and cultural expectations can create misunderstandings or slow progress. In these cases, the Scrum Master must not only remove practical impediments but also facilitate conflict resolution and improve communication among team members.

The ability to quickly recognize when communication problems arise and take steps to resolve them becomes a key competence for the Scrum Master in a heterogeneous environment. This may involve organizing more frequent clarification sessions or adapting collaboration tools to ensure that all members are involved and informed about critical decisions.

3.2.4 Building Trust in Heterogeneous Teams

Another important task for the Scrum Master in a heterogeneous context is building trust within the team. Trust is fundamental to the success of an agile team, as it facilitates open communication, constructive feedback, and swift problem resolution. However, building trust in distributed and diverse teams can be more challenging than in teams that work together physically.

The Scrum Master must invest time and energy in creating an environment where team members feel heard, respected, and valued, despite their different backgrounds. This can be achieved by organizing activities that foster mutual understanding, encouraging the sharing of experiences, and creating safe spaces where everyone can express their opinions without fear of judgment.

3.2.5 Adapting Tools and Practices

Finally, the Scrum Master must adapt agile tools and practices based on the specific needs of the heterogeneous team. This may involve using more advanced collaborative tools that allow for smooth and asynchronous communication or introducing new facilitation techniques that take into account differences in work styles and cultural preferences. The Scrum Master must be ready to experiment and modify the traditional agile process while keeping clear objectives and ensuring that the team remains productive.

3.2.6 Conclusion

In summary, the role of the Scrum Master in a heterogeneous team goes well beyond merely facilitating the agile process. They must become an intercultural mediator, an expert in remote communication, and a resolver of complex conflicts. Their ability to adapt and respond to the new dynamics of the team is crucial for ensuring that the group can operate cohesively and effectively despite the challenges posed by diversity and geographical distribution.

3.3 The Product Owner: Balancing Global Stakeholders

In the traditional agile context, the Product Owner is responsible for maximizing the value of the product and managing the product backlog, ensuring that the team works on activities that generate the greatest impact. This role requires close collaboration with both internal and external stakeholders, translating customer and market needs into clear priorities for the development team. However, in heterogeneous and global teams, the complexities increase significantly, requiring a Product Owner who can manage diverse priorities and expectations, often from stakeholders spread across multiple time zones, with different business cultures and local requirements.

3.3.1 Managing Stakeholders with Differing Priorities

In a traditional environment, the Product Owner may interact directly with a few stakeholders, often internal, who share similar goals and visions. However, in global or diversified contexts, the Product Owner must deal with a wide range of stakeholders who may have differing priorities, expectations, and success metrics. For example, stakeholders in one region may focus on speed to market, while others may prioritize product quality or compliance with specific regulations in that market.

The Product Owner must balance these differing priorities, often conflicting with one another, and turn them into a coherent and actionable roadmap for the development team. This requires not only the ability to negotiate and mediate but also a deep understanding of the cultural and business differences that drive these priorities. The Product Owner becomes a true "translator" between the needs of global stakeholders and the capabilities of the development team.

3.3.2 Adapting Communication

One of the most complex aspects of the Product Owner's role in a global team is managing communication. Intercultural communication requires a strong ability to adapt, as different stakeholders may have various communication styles and expectations regarding how information is shared, decisions are made, and priorities are managed.

In some cultural contexts, for instance, direct and transparent communication may be preferred, while in others, information might be conveyed in a more indirect and discreet manner. The Product Owner must navigate these differences, adapting their communication style to ensure that all stakeholders feel heard and understood. Additionally, in geographically distributed teams, the Product Owner often relies on digital tools to manage meetings and backlog reviews, using platforms such as Jira, Confluence, or Zoom to ensure that everyone can participate effectively, even if not at the same time.

3.3.3 Prioritizing in a Heterogeneous Context

Another crucial aspect for the Product Owner is prioritizing work in a heterogeneous context. When working with global stakeholders, the Product Owner may have to manage a backlog that includes different requests for products that must adapt to varying markets and regulations. The ability to balance local needs with the global vision of the product is essential.

For example, a Product Owner working with a team distributed between Asia and Europe may receive requests for different features to meet the specific needs of each market. In this case, the Product Owner must make decisions on which features to prioritize, balancing the potential value they can offer against the time and resources available to the team. This requires strong analytical skills and a clear strategic vision to ensure that today's choices do not compromise the future success of the product.

3.3.4 Reconciling Local and Global Visions

One of the most delicate tasks for the Product Owner in a global context is balancing a local vision with a global vision of the product. On one hand, local stakeholders may request customizations or specific adaptations for their markets, but on the other, the Product Owner must ensure that the product maintains global consistency and scalability. The ability to reconcile these two perspectives is essential to avoid product fragmentation that could compromise its quality or competitiveness on a global scale.

The Product Owner must have a clear understanding of global priorities while also being flexible enough to adapt certain features or characteristics to local needs, ensuring that differences are managed coherently and that the product remains sustainable in the long term.

3.3.5 Utilizing Tools and Metrics to Monitor Progress

In a global team, the Product Owner must have appropriate tools to monitor progress and evaluate the success of implemented features. The use of key performance indicators (KPIs) and analytical tools becomes fundamental to understand whether the team is moving in the right direction and whether the developed features are generating the expected value. In global contexts, these metrics can vary from one market to another, and the Product Owner must be able to collect and analyze data specific to each geographical area.

For example, the success of a feature might be measured in terms of customer satisfaction in one market and sales growth in another. Therefore, the Product Owner must manage and analyze a wide range of data, ensuring that success metrics are relevant for each context and can be translated into actionable steps for the team.

3.3.6 Building Trusting Relationships with Stakeholders

For a Product Owner working with distributed stakeholders, building trusting relationships is crucial for the project's success. Local stakeholders must feel involved and heard, even when their requests cannot be immediately met. The Product Owner must communicate clearly and transparently, explaining the reasons behind decisions and ensuring that each stakeholder understands how and when their priorities will be addressed.

This trust is built through constant communication, the use of collaborative tools, and the ability to actively listen to the needs of each stakeholder. In a heterogeneous context, this capacity for mediation and trust-building is essential to avoid conflicts and ensure that the development team can work productively.

3.3.7 Conclusion

In summary, the Product Owner in a global or heterogeneous context must be much more than a backlog manager. They must be a mediator between conflicting priorities, an expert in intercultural communication, and a strategic leader capable of balancing local and global visions. The ability to manage stakeholders with diverse needs, adapt communication, and maintain a clear and consistent vision of the product is crucial for the success of the team and the project.

3.4 The Development Team: Collaboration Among Diverse Disciplines and Skills

In the traditional agile framework, the development team is a cross-functional and self-organized group that works together to deliver functional product increments at the end of each sprint. This team typically consists of developers, testers, and other technical roles that collaborate closely to meet the requirements defined in the product backlog.

However, in heterogeneous teams, the concept of development broadens to include skills beyond just software development. The team may consist of marketing experts, designers, product specialists, researchers, and other professionals from diverse backgrounds, each with a distinct approach to their work.

This diversity creates new collaboration dynamics, necessitating an adaptation of the team to address the complexities of interactions across different disciplines and ensure that various skills integrate seamlessly.

3.4.1 Interdisciplinary Collaboration

In a traditional context, development teams tend to have similar, often technical, skills, which facilitates collaboration and communication. However, in a heterogeneous team, the presence of members with different skills and approaches (such as software developers, UX/UI designers, marketing experts, and product managers) introduces new challenges. Mutual understanding among different roles becomes crucial, as team members may have different goals, priorities, and professional languages.

For example, a developer might focus on technical aspects like code quality and system efficiency, while a designer might be more concerned with user experience and the aesthetics of the interface. A marketing expert, on the other hand, might primarily care about how the product will be positioned in the market and how it will meet customer needs. The success of a heterogeneous development team depends on these professionals' ability to collaborate effectively, sharing their expertise and aligning their priorities.

3.4.2 Structuring Communication to Facilitate Collaboration

Communication within a heterogeneous development team requires special attention. The diversity of disciplines and skills implies that team members may have different ways of approaching problems and making decisions. To avoid misunderstandings or conflicts, it's essential for the team to adopt practices of transparent and frequent communication. Digital tools, such as messaging channels (Slack, Microsoft Teams) or visual boards (Trello, Jira), can facilitate this communication, allowing all team members to stay updated on work progress and project priorities.

In a heterogeneous team, it is also important to organize regular alignment sessions where each member can present their progress in their area of work, discuss challenges they are facing, and receive feedback from others. These moments of exchange help ensure that everyone is on the same wavelength and that different disciplines work together cohesively.

3.4.3 Promoting Trust and Self-Organization

In the traditional agile context, the development team is self-organized, meaning that team members independently decide how to distribute the work and achieve the established goals. In heterogeneous teams, this self-organization can be more complex to implement, as diverse skills require greater coordination. However, the principle of self-organization remains crucial for the success of an agile team.

To promote self-organization in a heterogeneous team, it is essential to build trust among team members. Each professional must feel comfortable delegating tasks to other team members with complementary skills. Trust develops through ongoing collaboration and open communication, but it can also be strengthened through agile practices like retrospectives, where the team reflects on what has worked well and what can be improved without assigning blame.

3.4.4 Integrating Diverse Skills into the Development Process

In heterogeneous teams, a critical aspect is the integration of diverse skills into the product development cycle. In a team composed solely of developers, the development cycle is relatively linear: the backlog is defined, code is written, tested, and delivered. However, in a heterogeneous team, it is necessary for each skill to be involved at the appropriate phases of the project.

For example, a UX/UI designer should be involved in the early design phases to ensure that the interface is intuitive and user-friendly. Similarly, a marketing expert can provide valuable input on product positioning and customer needs, influencing technical development choices. The Scrum Master and the Product Owner must therefore work to ensure that all team members can participate in the process in a timely manner and that their skills are effectively utilized.

3.4.5 Resolving Conflicts Between Different Priorities

Members of a heterogeneous team may have different priorities and objectives depending on their area of expertise. For example, a designer may want to delay a delivery to perfect the user interface, while a marketer may be more focused on the need to launch the product quickly to seize a market opportunity. These conflicts can slow down the team's progress if not effectively addressed.

This is where the role of the Scrum Master or Product Owner comes into play, as they must mediate between these conflicting priorities and find a compromise that satisfies all parties. Utilizing tools such as backlog prioritization and holding open discussions during sprint planning can help ensure that the team remains focused on common goals while respecting the specific needs of different disciplines.

3.4.6 Supporting Continuous Improvement

Finally, in a heterogeneous development team, continuous improvement must be a priority. The team should have regular reflection moments, such as retrospectives, to identify what is working and what could be improved. In a team with diverse skills, these sessions can help overcome challenges in interdisciplinary collaboration, allowing the team to refine its practices and adapt to project needs.

The ability to learn from mistakes and continuously improve is fundamental to ensuring that a heterogeneous team can thrive. This learning process not only enhances the team's efficiency but also strengthens relationships among members, creating a culture of collaboration and innovation.

3.4.7 Conclusion

In summary, the development team in a heterogeneous context requires a more sophisticated approach to collaboration and communication compared to a traditional agile team. The diversity of skills and perspectives can be a significant asset but requires careful management to ensure that the team remains cohesive and productive. Trust, open communication, and the integration of diverse skills are the key elements for the success of a heterogeneous development team.

3.5 Adapting Roles to Team Needs

In a traditional agile team, the roles of Scrum Master, Product Owner, and Development Team are well-defined, each with specific and delineated responsibilities. However, in heterogeneous and complex teams, these delineations can become too rigid, necessitating a more flexible and adaptive approach to roles. In contexts where skills vary and work dynamics are more complex, it is often beneficial for team members to assume fluid roles and share or redistribute responsibilities differently than in traditional frameworks.

This adaptation of roles enables the team to better respond to changes and tackle challenges more collaboratively without losing the structure and clarity necessary to advance the project.

3.5.1 Flexibility in Roles

In a heterogeneous team, rigid roles can be counterproductive, as dynamics change based on project needs and team member skills. In these contexts, flexibility becomes a necessity. For instance, the Product Owner might need to work more closely with the Scrum Master to manage aspects related to communication with external stakeholders, while the Scrum Master may facilitate dialogue between different functions within the team, such as designers and developers.

This flexibility in roles does not necessarily imply an overlap or confusion of responsibilities but rather a continuous adaptation based on the specific needs of the project. Team members must be ready to wear "different hats" depending on the development phase and the moment's necessity.

3.5.2 Shared Responsibilities

In some heterogeneous teams, it may be beneficial to share certain responsibilities among multiple team members, especially when specific skills overlap or complement each other. For example, the Product Owner and the Development Team might share responsibility for managing the backlog, with the Product Owner setting strategic priorities while the team provides technical input to ensure that user stories are ready to be efficiently developed.

This sharing of responsibilities helps keep the team agile and responsive, allowing all members to actively participate in crucial project decisions. Collaboration among roles becomes a key factor for the team's success, especially when complex decisions require input from different perspectives.

3.5.3 Adapting to Team-Specific Skills

Every team is unique in terms of skills and knowledge, and role assignments must reflect these peculiarities. In a heterogeneous team, a member who would typically be part of the Development Team might temporarily take on some responsibilities of the Product Owner or Scrum Master based on their specific skills or experience. For example, an engineer with a strong understanding of business might assist the Product Owner in better translating business requirements into technical stories.

In this context, it is essential for the team to have a clear understanding of each member's competencies to redistribute responsibilities as needed without causing confusion or conflicts. Flexibility in role assignment allows the team to maximize everyone's abilities, improving the overall effectiveness of the work.

3.5.4 Temporary and Fluid Roles

An interesting approach in heterogeneous teams is the adoption of temporary or fluid roles, where team members assume different roles for short periods based on project needs. For example, during a phase of exploring new technologies or market research, a member of the Development Team might temporarily take on the role of facilitating communications with external stakeholders, borrowing some typical responsibilities of the Scrum Master.

This fluidity in roles allows the team to be more dynamic and to respond quickly to changes while maintaining a high level of organization. However, it is important that there is always adequate internal communication to ensure that everyone is aware of the temporary changes in roles and that there are no ambiguities regarding responsibilities.

3.5.5 Increased Interaction Between Scrum Master and Product Owner

In complex contexts, collaboration between the Scrum Master and Product Owner becomes even more crucial. While the two roles have distinct responsibilities, in heterogeneous teams, it can be beneficial for them to work together more closely. The Scrum Master can support the Product Owner in managing relationships with external stakeholders, especially in situations where rapid and continuous feedback is essential for project progress.

The Product Owner, on the other hand, can assist the Scrum Master in internal facilitation, ensuring that the team remains aligned with the product vision and that there are no ambiguities regarding priorities. This enhanced interaction between the two roles helps effectively manage the challenges arising from diverse and complex teams.

3.5.6 Active Involvement of All Members in Decision-Making

Another key element for adapting roles in a heterogeneous team is the importance of involving all team members in the decision-making process. Instead of limiting strategic and operational decisions to the Product Owner or Scrum Master, teams can benefit from greater collective participation in decisions, especially when they pertain to areas with highly diversified skills.

For instance, if a team is discussing new features to develop, it is useful to involve designers, engineers, and even marketing experts, as each brings a unique perspective that can enrich the final decision. The active involvement of all members strengthens self-organization and improves internal alignment.

3.5.7 Development of Distributed Leadership

Another evolution of roles in heterogeneous teams is the adoption of distributed leadership, where multiple team members assume leadership responsibilities at different times, depending on their skills and project needs. This approach not only makes the team more flexible but also encourages the professional development of members, allowing them to experience leadership roles without the pressure of having to hold them permanently.

Distributed leadership also creates greater resilience within the team, as responsibilities are not concentrated in a single person but are shared. This helps reduce the risks associated with dependence on a single leader and improves the team's ability to respond quickly to changes.

3.5.8 Conclusion: The Importance of Flexibility in Roles

In summary, in heterogeneous teams, adapting traditional roles is essential for ensuring success. Flexibility, shared responsibilities, and the adoption of fluid roles enable the team to better tackle the dynamic challenges of the project. In this context, the Scrum Master, Product Owner, and Development Team must be willing to evolve and take on complementary roles to ensure a smooth and productive workflow. This adaptability is fundamental for leveraging the diverse skills of the team and maintaining an agile approach even in the most complex contexts.

3.6 Communication in Teams

One of the most important and simultaneously complex elements to manage in a heterogeneous team is communication. In a traditional agile team, communication is generally facilitated by physical proximity and direct, constant interactions. However, in global or diverse teams, with members distributed geographically or belonging to different disciplines and cultures, maintaining clear and regular communication becomes a much more intricate challenge. The quality of communication can make the difference between the success and failure of an agile project.

3.6.1 The Challenge of Time Zones

One of the main obstacles in geographically distributed heterogeneous teams is managing time zones. In a global team, members may work at different times, making it difficult to schedule synchronous meetings such as daily standups or sprint planning sessions. This can lead to potential slowdowns in decision-making and information exchange, with some team members feeling excluded from critical discussions.

To overcome this obstacle, it is essential to adopt an asynchronous approach for many communication activities. Tools like Slack, Microsoft Teams, Loom, or task management platforms like Jira can be used to keep all team members updated, allowing them to participate in discussions and decisions even outside standard working hours. An alternative is to schedule rotating meetings that allow different members to participate at times that are fair to all, taking turns.

3.6.2 Language and Cultural Barriers

Another challenge in heterogeneous teams concerns language and cultural barriers. In international teams, language differences can lead to misunderstandings, miscommunications, and delays in communication. Even when all team members speak a common language, often English, the level of language proficiency can vary, creating further difficulties in understanding technical concepts or in strategic discussions.

Additionally, cultural differences can influence how people relate to one another, how they handle conflicts, and how they interpret verbal and non-verbal communication. Some team members may prefer more direct communication, while others may feel uncomfortable with explicit criticism or open discussions.

To address these barriers, the team must be aware of cultural differences and adapt its communication style. The Scrum Master plays a central role in facilitating this awareness, promoting inclusive communication practices and encouraging a work environment where all team members feel heard and understood. Moreover, using translation tools or providing written documentation in the preferred languages of team members can help reduce misunderstandings.

3.6.3 Utilizing Collaborative Tools

Online communication and collaboration tools are essential for keeping the team aligned. In addition to instant messaging channels like Slack and Microsoft Teams, implementing project management platforms like Jira, Trello, or Asana can help all team members keep track of activities, share updates, and monitor progress in real-time.

Video conferencing tools like Zoom or Google Meet are also vital for maintaining face-to-face interaction, albeit virtually. Video calls allow the team to stay connected and promote cohesion despite physical distance. However, it is important that such meetings are structured efficiently, considering that not all members may be available simultaneously due to time zone differences.

3.6.4 Creating Communication Rituals

In heterogeneous teams, it is essential to establish communication rituals that keep the team aligned, even in the absence of daily physical interactions. These rituals can include:

- Asynchronous Updates: Instead of holding a daily meeting, the team can update a dedicated channel with each member's progress, highlighting what has been done, any encountered problems, and the next steps.
- Weekly Syncs: More structured weekly meetings can be used to synchronize the team and resolve any issues or blockers.
- Sprint Reviews and Retrospectives: Standard end-of-sprint meetings to assess results and discuss areas for improvement. These can also be conducted asynchronously, with feedback provided via digital tools.

These rituals help maintain a constant flow of communication while respecting the diverse schedules and work styles of the team.

3.6.5 Transparency and Information Sharing

In a heterogeneous team, transparency is crucial to ensure that all members have access to relevant information and that there are no knowledge asymmetries. Tools like Confluence or Google Docs can be used to centralize documents, project plans, backlogs, and other important materials, ensuring that everyone has access to the same resources.

Moreover, information sharing should be structured to allow for easy understanding and traceability. It is useful for the team to adopt practices such as continuous documentation, where every significant change is recorded and made available to the entire team. This reduces the risk of misunderstandings or errors due to a lack of information.

3.6.6 Resolving Communication Conflicts

In heterogeneous teams, conflicts may arise due to cultural differences, diverging expectations, or linguistic misunderstandings. The Scrum Master plays a crucial role in resolving conflicts, facilitating communication among team members and promoting a positive work environment. It is essential to address conflicts constructively and promptly before they become significant obstacles to project progress.

The Product Owner and the Development Team should be involved in the discussion, ensuring that all parties are heard and that decisions are made transparently.

Establishing a culture of open and respectful feedback can help prevent and resolve conflicts before they harm team collaboration.

Conclusion

In summary, effective communication is vital in heterogeneous teams, where traditional communication methods may not suffice. By understanding the challenges posed by time zones, language barriers, and cultural differences, teams can adopt strategies to enhance communication and collaboration. Utilizing collaborative tools, creating communication rituals, promoting transparency, and resolving conflicts constructively will help ensure that all team members remain engaged and aligned in their efforts. In doing so, heterogeneous teams can thrive and achieve their project goals successfully.

3.7 Cross-Functional Skills in Heterogeneous Teams

In a traditional agile team, each member is responsible for their technical work, and roles are clear and well-defined. However, in a heterogeneous team, where different competencies, disciplines, and cultures coexist, cross-functional skills become essential to ensure project success. These skills, also known as soft skills, include effective communication, conflict management, intercultural sensitivity, collaborative leadership, and the ability to adapt quickly to changes. In heterogeneous teams, technical skills alone are not enough; team members must be capable of working harmoniously together despite their differences.

3.7.1 Effective Communication as the Foundation of Collaboration

In a heterogeneous team, effective communication is one of the most important cross-functional skills. Team members must be able to clearly explain their ideas and actively listen to others, especially when there are language or cultural differences. Effective communication is not limited to verbal interactions but also includes the ability to use digital tools for remote collaboration, writing clear documentation, and adapting one's communication style to meet the needs of other team members.

In a distributed context, it is crucial that communication is structured and that feedback is timely and constructive. A Scrum Master or Product Owner who masters this skill can better facilitate interactions among team members, promoting an environment where everyone feels heard and valued.

3.7.2 Intercultural Sensitivity

Intercultural sensitivity is another key competency in heterogeneous teams. Every culture has different expectations regarding how work should be conducted, communicated, and conflicts resolved. In international teams, it is common for members to come from very different cultural backgrounds, with work styles that can vary significantly. For instance, some may prefer a hierarchical and direct approach to problem-solving, while others may opt for a more collaborative and democratic method.

The ability to recognize these differences and adapt one's behavior to respect the cultural expectations of others is fundamental to creating a cohesive team. The Scrum Master plays a crucial role in fostering intercultural understanding within the team, ensuring that diverse cultural perspectives are taken into account and valued.

3.7.3 Conflict Management

In heterogeneous teams, conflicts can arise more easily due to cultural differences, varying expectations, or different work styles. The ability to manage these conflicts constructively is an indispensable cross-functional skill to prevent tensions from damaging team productivity. The Scrum Master and Product Owner must be adept at recognizing signs of potential conflicts and intervening quickly to mediate differences.

Conflict management involves not only resolving disagreements but also facilitating difficult conversations and turning conflict into an opportunity for team improvement. This requires emotional intelligence, empathy, and active listening skills.

3.7.4 Collaborative Leadership

In a heterogeneous team, collaborative leadership is essential to guide the group without imposing rigid authority. In agile contexts, leadership is not concentrated in one person but is distributed among team members, allowing everyone to have a voice and contribute to the decision-making process. The ability to inspire and motivate the team without exerting excessive control is a skill that requires balance.

The Scrum Master and Product Owner must demonstrate leadership that encourages autonomy and shared responsibility. In heterogeneous teams, this competency becomes even more critical, as team members may have different experiences and backgrounds regarding what it means to be a leader. Distributed leadership helps engage everyone in the process and fosters a culture of mutual respect.

3.7.5 Adaptability

The ability to adapt quickly to changes is a crucial skill in agile teams but becomes even more important in heterogeneous teams. Working with people from different disciplines, backgrounds, and locations requires considerable mental flexibility. Team members must be ready to change approaches, tools, or processes based on the project's needs and the group's dynamics.

In a heterogeneous team, changes may occur more frequently, and the ability to embrace these changes positively and proactively is essential for maintaining the team's agility and effectiveness. The Scrum Master plays an important role in guiding the team through these transitions and keeping motivation high, even when circumstances change rapidly.

3.7.6 Empathy and Emotional Intelligence

Empathy and emotional intelligence are essential cross-functional skills for understanding the feelings and concerns of other team members. In heterogeneous teams, where differences can amplify misunderstandings, the ability to "put oneself in others' shoes" becomes an indispensable quality. This not only improves collaboration but also fosters an inclusive work environment where every team member feels respected and valued.

The Product Owner and Scrum Master must be able to pick up on emotional cues from team members, helping them overcome frustrations or personal difficulties that could impact group work. Promoting a culture of listening and mutual understanding is crucial for the well-being of the team.

3.7.7 Critical Thinking and Problem Solving

Finally, a key cross-functional skill in heterogeneous teams is the ability to solve problems critically and collaboratively. In agile teams, problem-solving cannot be limited to one person or group; it must be shared. Every team member should be capable of analyzing situations, proposing solutions, and collaborating to resolve issues quickly.

In a heterogeneous team, diverse skills and perspectives can offer creative new solutions to problems, but only if members are willing to work together constructively. Promoting critical thinking and collaboration in problem-solving is a shared responsibility among all team members, but the Scrum Master and Product Owner must ensure that the process is facilitated effectively.

3.7.8 Conclusion

Cross-functional skills are essential for the success of heterogeneous teams. The ability to communicate effectively, manage conflicts, adapt to changes, and work collaboratively are all skills that, when developed and encouraged, can transform a heterogeneous team into a high-performing unit. The Scrum Master and Product Owner play a key role in cultivating these skills, creating an inclusive and cohesive work environment where differences are not only accepted but viewed as an opportunity for innovation and continuous improvement.

Chapter 3 – Clear Roles and Responsibilities

Chapter 4

Integration of Methodologies

Chapter 4 – Integration of Methodologies

4.1 Challenges of Integrating Different Agile Frameworks

Integrating multiple agile frameworks like Scrum, Kanban, and Extreme Programming (XP) is a common practice in many companies seeking to leverage the best from each approach. However, this integration presents numerous challenges, particularly in heterogeneous teams, where cultural, skill, and expectation differences can make the combination of agile methods complex and confusing.

When integrating different methodologies, there is often hope that each framework can bring its specific benefits to the project. For example, Scrum provides a clear structure with fixed work cycles, Kanban allows for more flexible and continuous workflow management, and XP introduces rigorous technical practices that improve code quality. However, these methodologies do not always combine seamlessly, especially if there is no well-defined strategy on how and when to apply each framework.

4.1.1 Differences in Approach and Structure

One of the first challenges that arise when integrating different frameworks concerns differences in approach and structure. Scrum is highly structured, with well-defined roles and events (such as sprint planning, daily scrum, and retrospective). These regular alignment moments are designed to foster collaboration and team self-organization. In contrast, Kanban relies on a continuous workflow without fixed sprint cycles, allowing teams to pull in new tasks based on their capacity, without the need for rigid planning.

This difference can create confusion among team members who may not know which approach to follow. For instance, some members may feel comfortable with the structure of Scrum, while others prefer the flexibility of Kanban. Without clear guidance on when to apply each framework, the risk is that the team is not aligned, with some following the Scrum flow and others working more flexibly with Kanban, leading to inefficiencies and a lack of coherence.

4.1.2 Confusion in Roles and Responsibilities

Another challenge in integrating agile frameworks is the confusion in roles and responsibilities. For example, in Scrum, the roles of the Scrum Master, Product Owner, and Development Team are clearly defined, each with a specific set of responsibilities. However, integration with Kanban or XP can lead to overlaps or uncertainties regarding roles.

In Kanban, there are no formal roles as in Scrum, which can lead to misunderstandings about who is responsible for what. If team members do not have a clear understanding of their tasks and responsibilities in a hybrid context, it may result in some activities being overlooked or, conversely, managed by multiple people, creating redundancies. In heterogeneous teams, where communication is already complicated by cultural or linguistic barriers, this lack of clarity can amplify issues.

4.1.3 Overload of Events and Tools

Integrating multiple agile frameworks can lead to an overload of events and tools. For example, a team attempting to combine Scrum and Kanban might find themselves managing both daily Scrum meetings and the continuous workflow of Kanban, without a clear separation between the two approaches. This can lead to redundant meetings or excessive monitoring of work, slowing down the team instead of enhancing its efficiency.

Similarly, using different tools to support each framework (e.g., a Scrum board for sprints and a Kanban board for continuous flow management) can further complicate the process, causing the team to waste time managing multiple platforms rather than delivering work. In heterogeneous teams, where members may have different levels of familiarity with technological tools, this overload can lead to frustration and inefficiency.

4.1.4 Risk of Losing Focus

When attempting to combine multiple agile frameworks, there is also a risk of losing focus. Each agile methodology has its strengths, but it also has practices that require dedication and attention to be effective. For example, Scrum requires strict adherence to sprints and review meetings, while XP emphasizes technical practices like pair programming and automated testing.

Trying to integrate these practices into a single approach can lead to a situation where the team ends up not fully adhering to either methodology, thus missing out on the benefits of each. In heterogeneous teams, where collaborative dynamics are already more complex, the lack of clear focus can lead to decreased productivity and frustration among team members.

4.1.5 Need for Strong Leadership

To overcome these challenges, strong leadership is essential to guide the team through the process of integrating agile frameworks. The Scrum Master and Product Owner must have a deep understanding of each framework and its applications and must be able to adapt practices to the specific needs of the project and team members.

It is important to establish clear guidelines on when to apply each framework and how the various roles and responsibilities integrate. In heterogeneous teams, leadership must also facilitate communication among members, ensuring that everyone has a clear understanding of the process and objectives. Additionally, a culture of continuous feedback should be encouraged, where the team can regularly reflect on the effectiveness of framework integration and make necessary adjustments.

4.1.6 Conclusion

In summary, integrating different agile frameworks offers many opportunities to improve team flexibility and effectiveness, but it also presents numerous challenges, especially in heterogeneous contexts. Without clear guidance and constant attention to team alignment, integration can lead to confusion, inefficiency, and loss of focus. However, with strong leadership and a well-defined strategy, it is possible to successfully combine the practices of Scrum, Kanban, XP, and other frameworks, creating a tailored approach that meets the needs of the project and the team.

4.2 The Importance of Clear Guidance

One of the main success factors in integrating different agile frameworks is having clear guidance that defines how and when to apply each approach. In heterogeneous teams, this guidance becomes even more crucial, as the variety of skills, cultural backgrounds, and familiarity with various agile methods can lead to misunderstandings and misalignments. Without explicit direction, the risk is that team members do not have a clear picture of which practices to adopt at specific times, leading to confusion, inefficiencies, and loss of focus.

4.2.1 Defining When to Apply Each Framework

The first challenge is deciding when and how to use the different frameworks. For example, a company may choose to use Scrum for complex, long-term projects, where the structure of sprints and regular planning helps keep the team aligned and measure progress iteratively. On the other hand, for more operational or maintenance activities, such as managing incoming requests, Kanban may be more suitable, offering flexibility and allowing for quick responses to changes without the rigidity of sprints.

Without clear guidance establishing in which contexts to use each framework, team members may end up applying Scrum practices in situations where Kanban would be more efficient, or vice versa, leading to inappropriate use of methodologies. It is therefore essential that the Scrum Master or Product Owner define clear criteria for determining which approach to adopt based on the specific needs of the project.

4.2.2 Coordinating Expectations among Team Members

Another critical aspect of guidance is coordinating expectations. In heterogeneous teams, members may have different experiences with the various agile frameworks. Some may be very experienced in Scrum, while others may be more accustomed to working with Kanban or Extreme Programming (XP). This difference in personal experiences can lead to misunderstandings about how each framework should be implemented and what the team's expectations are regarding the processes.

To prevent misalignments, the guidance should not only explain which frameworks to adopt but also how to align the expectations of all team members. This can be done through joint training sessions, workshops, and open discussions on how each methodology will be used in the project. Creating a common foundation of knowledge and expectations helps avoid conflicts and ensures that all team members are on the same wavelength.

4.2.3 Establishing Clear Roles and Responsibilities

Confusion about roles and responsibilities can become a serious issue in teams trying to integrate different agile frameworks. In Scrum, the roles of the Scrum Master, Product Owner, and Development Team are well defined and separated, but when integrating other frameworks like Kanban or XP, these distinctions can become less clear.

Clear guidance should include a detailed mapping of the roles and responsibilities of each team member based on the adopted frameworks. For example, in a team using Scrum for development and Kanban for managing operations, the Product Owner might maintain control of the overall backlog, while the Scrum Master facilitates Scrum events and helps manage Kanban activities. In such a hybrid approach, it is important that each team member understands their tasks at each phase of the process to avoid overlaps or operational gaps.

4.2.4 Providing Strong Leadership

In heterogeneous teams, strong leadership is essential to ensure that the clear guidance is followed and that the integration of frameworks proceeds smoothly. The role of the Scrum Master becomes even more central in a context of integration, as they must not only facilitate the agile process but also help the team navigate between different methodological practices, ensuring that the focus remains on outcomes.

Leadership must also be able to adapt to the team's needs, especially in heterogeneous contexts where dynamics may be more complex. The Product Owner and Scrum Master must work together to make quick decisions and resolve any issues that may arise during the integration of frameworks. This may include the need for specific retrospectives to discuss the effectiveness of the framework combination, to understand what works and what needs improvement.

4.2.5 Avoiding Excessive Rigidity

While having clear guidance is essential, it is equally important to avoid excessive rigidity in applying the frameworks. The integration of agile frameworks must be flexible enough to allow the team to adapt to changing circumstances and project needs. For example, it might be necessary to use Scrum during the initial phases of product development to give the team a defined structure and objectives, and then switch to a more Kanban approach once the product is in maintenance and requires quicker responses to incoming issues.

The guidance should thus provide guidelines to help the team make informed decisions while also allowing room for adaptation, so the team can modify its approach as project needs evolve. Flexible guidance enables heterogeneous teams to experiment and find the right balance among the various frameworks.

4.2.6 Conclusion

In summary, clear guidance is essential to ensure the success of integrating different agile frameworks, especially in heterogeneous teams. Defining when and how to apply each framework, coordinating expectations among team members, and establishing clear roles and responsibilities are crucial elements to avoid confusion and inefficiency. At the same time, strong leadership and some flexibility in guidance allow the team to adapt and respond effectively to changes while always maintaining focus on final outcomes.

4.3 Case Study: A Multicultural Tech Startup

To illustrate the difficulties and complexities of integrating agile frameworks in a heterogeneous context, we examine the case of a multicultural tech startup. This company operates globally, with teams distributed across Europe, Asia, and North America, each with different approaches, habits, and cultural backgrounds. The company decided to combine Scrum and Kanban to improve both the development of new products and the ongoing management of operations.

4.3.1. Cultural and Approach Misalignment

In this startup, the European teams were already experienced in using Scrum, working in fixed sprints with daily meetings and regular retrospectives. On the other hand, the Asian team, accustomed to a more fluid workflow, preferred the Kanban approach, with less emphasis on structured events and rigid deadlines. This misalignment caused confusion among team members, who did not know when to use one method over the other or how to balance the pressure of sprints with the continuous flow of Kanban.

4.3.2. Synchronization Issues

Further complicating the situation was the geographic distribution and the different time zones. Scrum daily meetings, such as the daily stand-up, were held at times that were not compatible with the availability of the Asian team, reducing their participation and creating a lack of alignment among team members. The team in Asia followed the Kanban flow continuously, while the team in Europe was constrained by the timing of Scrum sprints. This led to delays and misunderstandings in deliveries, with issues that could have been resolved quickly if the team had more effective synchronization moments.

4.3.3. Leadership Adaptation

To resolve these issues, the leadership of the startup decided to reassess the integration of frameworks, adopting a more structured hybrid approach. They implemented Scrum for developing new features, maintaining standard events such as sprint planning and retrospectives, but allowed maintenance activities to follow the Kanban flow, where requests were managed continuously. Additionally, they introduced a rotation of stand-up meetings to ensure that each team had the opportunity to participate in daily discussions, thus creating constant alignment.

4.3.4. Case Conclusion

This case highlights how, in a multicultural context, combining multiple agile frameworks can lead to misalignments and inefficiencies if not managed with clear guidance and adaptive leadership. The flexibility in applying frameworks and the ability to adapt events and tools to different cultural and geographical contexts were fundamental in resolving issues and improving the workflow of the startup.

4.4 Adapting Frameworks to Local and Global Needs

In the context of heterogeneous teams, such as that of the multicultural tech startup in the case study, it is crucial to understand that there is no single agile framework that can perfectly meet all needs. Flexibility and the ability to adapt frameworks to specific local and global requirements become key elements in maintaining operational effectiveness and alignment among team members.

4.4.1. Local Needs in Distributed Teams

Each team, based on its geographical location and cultural context, may have different expectations and operational priorities. For example, the Asian team of the startup had a less structured and more adaptive approach thanks to the use of Kanban, which suited their need to respond quickly to local market changes and operational requests. On the other hand, the European team, more accustomed to rigorous planning, found the structure of Scrum more useful for maintaining a clear long-term direction.

Local adaptation allowed the startup to differentiate the use of frameworks: using Scrum for managing more complex projects and an iterative workflow pipeline, and Kanban for local needs of rapid and continuous response to requests.

4.4.2. Integrating the Global Vision with Local Needs

One of the biggest challenges in adapting frameworks is ensuring that distributed teams maintain global alignment on the strategic objectives of the company. While adopting different practices, teams must ensure that their work is consistent with the overall vision of the organization. The leadership of the startup had to balance operational flexibility with the need for corporate consistency, establishing common processes for reviewing objectives and sharing results.

For example, while teams followed different frameworks, the startup implemented shared events, such as the global sprint review, where progress was presented in a common context. This ensured that, despite local differences, all teams remained focused on the main corporate objectives.

4.4.3. Lesson Learned: Flexibility and Standardization

The case of the startup demonstrates the importance of balancing local flexibility with a certain level of global standardization. The specific operational needs of each team were respected through the use of different frameworks, but leadership maintained a minimum level of standardization to ensure that results were measurable and comparable on a global scale. This combination allowed leveraging the advantages of various frameworks while adapting them to the specific needs of each team without losing overall cohesion.

4.4.4. Conclusion

Adapting agile frameworks to local and global needs requires a balanced approach that considers the cultural and operational dynamics of each team. The ability to modulate the application of agile methodologies, without sacrificing the overall vision of the company, enables heterogeneous teams to work efficiently while maintaining strategic alignment on a global scale.

4.5 Reducing Uncertainty through Standardization

In a context where different agile frameworks are integrated, a significant risk is the uncertainty that team members may perceive regarding the practices to follow. This risk is amplified in heterogeneous teams, where cultural and skill differences can increase misunderstandings. To reduce this uncertainty, many companies adopt a partial standardization approach, which allows for maintaining some consistency in processes while leaving room for the flexibility required by various local contexts.

4.5.1. Standardization of Core Practices

One of the most effective strategies to reduce uncertainty is to establish core practices common to all teams, regardless of the framework used. For example, even if one team uses Scrum and another Kanban, both can share the same method of managing the backlog, maintaining a clear and easy-to-follow structure. Standardizing these critical aspects reduces confusion and allows all team members to have a common foundation to rely on.

Another area where standardization is beneficial is the adoption of shared events. Even in teams using different frameworks, practices such as retrospectives or daily stand-ups can be maintained, providing regular moments of comparison and alignment. This helps keep communication open and quickly address any issues or misalignments.

4.5.2. Minimizing the Risk of Operational Divergence

In the absence of some standardization, there is a risk that teams may take divergent operational paths, creating inefficiencies and slowdowns. When each team has the freedom to adopt different practices without clear guidelines, methodologies can be applied in very different ways, leading to a fragmentation of the process. This risk is particularly high in heterogeneous teams, where the lack of standard guidance can amplify cultural and operational differences.

To minimize this risk, the tech startup in the case study decided to standardize the use of work management tools like Jira, ensuring that all teams worked with the same platform while maintaining flexibility in the application of various frameworks. This way, each team had the freedom to choose the practices that best met their needs, but operational transparency was maintained through the use of a shared tool.

4.5.3. Standardization as a Basis for Continuous Improvement

In addition to reducing uncertainty, partial standardization facilitates continuous improvement. When teams share common practices and tools, it is easier to identify areas for improvement and implement solutions that can be applied on a global scale. The retrospectives common to all teams allowed the startup in the case study to regularly analyze the effectiveness of processes and consistently adapt practices.

This continuous improvement process, based on a standard foundation, enables rapid scaling of best practices across teams. If one team finds an effective solution to a specific problem, that solution can be implemented more easily in other teams, thus reducing adaptation times and improving the overall effectiveness of the organization.

4.5.4. Conclusion

Standardization, when applied partially and strategically, reduces uncertainty in heterogeneous teams and allows for maintaining a minimum level of consistency without sacrificing the operational flexibility necessary in different contexts. Through the standardization of core practices and the use of common tools, companies can improve efficiency, reduce risks of operational divergence, and facilitate continuous improvement on a global scale.

4.6 Conclusion

The integration of different agile frameworks in heterogeneous teams can bring numerous advantages but also poses significant challenges that require careful management and a well-defined strategy. As seen in the case of the multicultural tech startup, combining methodologies like Scrum and Kanban can be an effective solution to meet local and global needs. However, without clear guidance and strong leadership, this integration risks creating confusion, misalignments, and inefficiencies.

4.6.1. The Need for Flexibility and Standardization

One of the key lessons that emerged from the integration of frameworks is the need to balance flexibility and standardization. While each team has different operational and cultural needs, it is essential to maintain a foundation of common processes and tools to ensure that work is transparent and coordinated on a global scale. Partial standardization, such as using shared tools and adopting common core practices, helps reduce uncertainty and prevent fragmentation of processes.

4.6.2. The Role of Leadership

Success in integrating agile methodologies heavily depends on leadership. Product Owners and Scrum Masters must be able to guide the team through the challenges related to integration, ensuring that the frameworks are applied correctly and adapted to the needs of the project and context. It is crucial for leadership to maintain a focus on strategic alignment, ensuring that local differences do not compromise the company's global objectives.

4.6.3. Continuity and Adaptation

Finally, the key to successfully managing a hybrid approach in heterogeneous teams is continuous adaptation. The needs of the team and the project change over time, and agile frameworks must evolve accordingly. Through a continuous feedback cycle and regular retrospectives, companies can constantly refine their practices, integrating frameworks in a way that responds to emerging challenges and improves team effectiveness.

4.6.4. Final Conclusion

Integrating different agile frameworks requires a strategic vision but also a high level of adaptability. In heterogeneous teams, where cultural, operational, and geographical differences can amplify difficulties, clear guidance, intelligent use of standardization, and strong leadership are essential to keep the team aligned and productive. With a well-balanced approach, companies can leverage the advantages of various agile methodologies, responding more effectively to global and local challenges.

Chapter 4 – Integration of Methodologies

Chapter 5
Evaluation of ROI in the Adoption of Agile Methodologies

Chapter 5 – Evaluation of ROI in the Adoption of Agile Methodologies

In this chapter, we will explore the return on investment (ROI) derived from the adoption of agile methodologies in general, with particular attention to the challenges and hidden costs that emerge when agility is imposed on heterogeneous teams composed of members with different backgrounds, skills, and cultures. Agility, when applied correctly, can lead to significant improvements in efficiency and responsiveness to the market, but these methodologies are not without difficulties when faced with complex and varied contexts.

5.1 ROI of Agility: Expected Benefits

The adoption of agile methodologies is often justified by the numerous benefits they can bring to organizations. Generally, the most cited advantages when adopting an agile framework, such as Scrum, Kanban, or XP, include:

• Increased Productivity: Agility allows projects to be broken down into smaller, manageable iterations, enabling teams to deliver value more quickly. This continuous cycle of delivery and feedback helps improve productivity, as the team can address and resolve issues iteratively, avoiding large rework at the end of the project.

• Greater Flexibility and Adaptability: One of the fundamental advantages of agility is the ability to quickly adapt to changes. Agile, with its iterative cycles and emphasis on continuous feedback, enables teams to respond to changing market or customer needs without having to completely redesign the project.

• Collaboration and Transparency: Agile methodologies promote open and frequent communication among team members and between the team and stakeholders. Working transparently helps to quickly identify issues and ensures that everyone is aligned on goals, improving cooperation and reducing internal conflicts.

• Improvement in Product Quality: With practices like continuous delivery and frequent testing, issues are identified and resolved promptly, before they become critical. This leads to a higher-quality final product, with fewer bugs and more refined features.

However, these benefits can vary widely depending on the context and the team's ability to correctly implement agile frameworks. In heterogeneous teams, in particular, it is important to consider the contextual factors that may influence the achievement of these results.

5.2 Challenges and Hidden Costs of Adopting Agility in Heterogeneous Teams

Despite the widely advertised benefits of agile methodologies, the adoption of these frameworks in heterogeneous teams poses a series of challenges and hidden costs that can significantly reduce the expected ROI. These difficulties often emerge when companies do not adequately consider the specifics of teams with differing cultural, linguistic, or technical backgrounds.

5.2.1. Resistance to Change

One of the most evident costs in adopting agility is the resistance to change from team members, especially in environments where traditional or structured work is deeply rooted. In heterogeneous teams, this resistance can be amplified by cultural differences. For example, team members from more hierarchical or formal cultures may find it difficult to adapt to an agile work method that encourages autonomy and individual responsibility. This slows down adoption and requires greater investments in training and coaching, which in turn increases the overall project costs.

5.2.2. Complex Communication

Communication is another significant challenge. In global or distributed teams, linguistic and cultural differences can cause misunderstandings, leading to delays or errors. Agile practices rely on constant and fluid communication among team members, but in a heterogeneous context, this can be difficult to achieve. The extra time spent resolving misunderstandings and managing expectations can increase coordination costs, eroding ROI.

5.2.3. Integration of Frameworks

In many heterogeneous teams, integrating different agile frameworks is common. However, combining Scrum, Kanban, or XP without a clear strategy can create confusion among team members, leading to an overload of processes and decreased efficiency. The lack of a clear distinction on when to use one framework over another can cause misalignments and slow down the development cycle.

5.2.4. High Coordination Costs

In heterogeneous teams, coordination among members becomes more complex and time-consuming, increasing operational costs. Frequent meetings, necessary alignments across different time zones, and managing teams with diverse skills and backgrounds can overload the agile process. These hidden costs are not always considered during the planning phase but can significantly impact the overall ROI of the project.

5.2.5. Conflicts of Priorities and Goals

Finally, in teams with heterogeneous skills or backgrounds, conflicts often arise regarding how to address project priorities. Team members may have differing opinions on which tasks are most important or how to allocate resources, leading to decision-making delays and inefficiencies.

5.2.6. Conclusion

In summary, while agility offers significant potential benefits, the heterogeneous context introduces hidden costs that can erode expected gains. Addressing these costs requires careful management, investments in communication and training, and particular attention to the seamless integration of various agile frameworks to ensure that the team remains aligned and productive.

5.3. When Agility is Forced: Negative Impact on ROI

One of the most common mistakes companies make is forcing the adoption of agile methodologies in contexts where they are not fully understood or suitable. This is especially true in heterogeneous teams, where cultural, operational, and experiential differences can amplify the problems associated with forced implementation. The impact of this coercion can be devastating on the expected ROI, leading to inefficiencies, dissatisfaction, and even a deterioration in the overall performance of the team.

5.3.1. Reduced Motivation

When agility is imposed from above without a shared understanding of its principles, team members may perceive it as a bureaucratic constraint. Instead of seeing the benefits in terms of autonomy and continuous improvement, the methodology is viewed as another set of rules to follow, reducing motivation. In heterogeneous teams, where resistance to change may be more pronounced, this imposition can generate frustration, leading to decreased engagement and, consequently, reduced productivity.

5.3.2. Inadequate Processes

Not all projects or teams benefit from adopting iterative methodologies. For example, in sectors with more linear or regulated needs, such as manufacturing or financial services, an agile approach can be counterproductive. Forcing a team to work with Scrum or Kanban when tasks require more sequential processes can lead to confusion and inefficiencies. In these cases, instead of improving flexibility and execution speed, the team risks wasting time trying to adapt to a framework that does not align with real operational needs.

5.3.3. Overload of Practices and Tools

In heterogeneous teams, the introduction of agile methodologies can often add to pre-existing practices and processes. This overload leads to a duplication of activities, with teams having to manage both old methods and new ones without a clear transition. The adoption of too many tools or practices in parallel can make work fragmented and chaotic, slowing down the execution of daily tasks and decreasing focus on primary objectives. The result is a negative ROI, as the time spent managing practices outweighs the added value derived from adopting agility.

5.3.4. Difficulty in Managing Change

Forcing the adoption of agility in contexts where the team is not ready to handle change can lead to a lack of understanding of new practices. Corporate leadership, in an attempt to quickly implement agility, may underestimate the importance of the time needed for training and cultural adaptation of the team. This accelerates internal resistance, hindering the effective adoption of methodologies and drastically reducing ROI.

5.3.5. Conclusion

Forcing the adoption of agility on unprepared teams or in contexts where it is not suitable can have a significant negative impact on ROI. Instead of delivering benefits such as speed and flexibility, forced agility can result in decreased motivation, ineffective processes, and an overload of practices, ultimately worsening the overall performance of the team.

5.4. Maximizing ROI through Agile Adaptation

To achieve the maximum return on investment (ROI) from adopting agile methodologies, it is essential to adapt agility to the specific needs of heterogeneous teams and the business context. Implementing agile practices flexibly and contextually, rather than rigidly, can ensure that the team benefits from the methodologies without sacrificing operational effectiveness. Here are some key strategies to maximize ROI:

5.4.1. Adapting Agile Frameworks to Local Contexts

In heterogeneous teams, each group may find itself working in different cultural, geographical, and professional contexts. Instead of imposing a single, rigid agile framework, it is more productive to customize agile practices based on local dynamics. For example, in a team with members distributed across various parts of the world, it may be necessary to modify the frequency of agile events, such as daily stand-ups, to accommodate time zones or the working rhythms of each group.

This flexibility allows teams to use what works best for them while remaining aligned with agile principles. Adapting the framework does not mean abandoning agility but ensuring that it operates realistically and practically for each operational context.

5.4.2. Investing in Continuous Training

To overcome cultural, technical, or resistance-to-change barriers, it is crucial to invest in continuous training. In heterogeneous teams, members may have varying levels of familiarity with agile methodologies. Training not only helps standardize skills but also fosters a shared culture based on agile principles.

Additionally, continuous training ensures that agile methodologies can evolve with the team. Ongoing learning allows for identifying weaknesses in framework adoption and progressively improving, thereby optimizing ROI in the long term.

5.4.3. Reducing Hidden Costs through Effective Management

Conscious project management is essential for reducing hidden costs that may arise from integrating agile practices in heterogeneous teams. Meeting overload, confusion about roles and responsibilities, and coordination issues can be mitigated by adopting collaboration tools that support asynchronous work and streamline communication among distributed members.

Another effective strategy is to simplify workflows by eliminating redundant practices or unnecessary tools that can slow down the team. For instance, adopting a single platform for task management, like Jira, can provide transparency and clarity, reducing coordination costs and increasing productivity.

5.4.4. Flexibility in Leadership

Agile leadership must be flexible and open to continuous adaptation. In heterogeneous teams, leaders' ability to guide change, maintain focus on objectives, and resolve challenges related to team diversity is crucial to ensuring the effectiveness of agile practices. A flexible Product Owner or Scrum Master can adapt the management of priorities and events to better meet local needs, thus maximizing ROI.

5.4.5. Conclusion

To maximize ROI in adopting agility in heterogeneous teams, it is crucial to adopt a flexible and adaptive approach. Customizing agile frameworks, investing in continuous training, and maintaining conscious management are all factors that can reduce hidden costs and enhance team effectiveness. By adapting agile practices to the unique context of each team, companies can fully leverage agile methodologies, thereby improving long-term investment returns.

5.5. Conclusion: A More Informed ROI

Evaluating the return on investment (ROI) from adopting agile methodologies in heterogeneous teams requires a broader and more informed perspective on the dynamics at play. While agile methodologies promise benefits in terms of efficiency, speed of delivery, and product quality, applying these practices in complex and diverse contexts introduces a series of challenges and hidden costs that must be carefully considered.

5.5.1. A Broader Evaluation of ROI

It's not enough to calculate ROI based solely on productivity or development speed metrics. It's crucial to include operational costs associated with managing the complexity of heterogeneous teams, such as coordination costs, ongoing training, and managing cultural and skill differences. These elements can directly influence ROI and must be continuously monitored to understand whether agility is truly delivering the expected benefits.

5.5.2. Recognizing Hidden Costs

To achieve a more informed ROI, companies must be willing to recognize and address the hidden costs associated with adopting agility. Investing in training and managing differences among team members is essential to ensure that agile methodologies are not only implemented but understood and applied correctly. Ignoring these costs can drastically reduce the benefits of agility and turn adoption into a costly failure.

5.5.3. Continuous Adaptation

Continuous adaptation of agile practices to the specific needs of heterogeneous teams is another key element for maximizing ROI. Rather than adopting a rigid and universal approach, organizations must be prepared to modify and refine their use of agile methodologies based on the unique circumstances of each team. This type of flexibility ensures that agility remains relevant and useful, thus maximizing returns on investment over time.

5.5.4. The Role of Leadership

Finally, a positive ROI largely depends on agile leadership. Leaders who can adapt, communicate effectively, and guide the team through necessary changes can make a significant difference in the success of agile adoption. Leadership that understands and embraces the complex dynamics of heterogeneous teams will be able to maintain focus on business objectives and long-term strategic benefits.

5.5.5. Final Conclusion

In summary, the ROI of agility cannot be measured solely in terms of speed or immediate efficiency. It must include a comprehensive assessment of hidden costs and operational difficulties that may arise in heterogeneous teams. With strong leadership, continuous adaptation, and a conscious view of costs, companies can maximize returns on investment, ensuring that agile methodologies deliver tangible and sustainable benefits in the long run.

SECTION 2: *Agility in Heterogeneous Contexts – Challenges and Opportunities*

Chapter 6

The Moments of Agility in Heterogeneous Teams- More than Events, a True Momentum

Chapter 6 – The Moments of Agility in Heterogeneous Teams - More than Events, a True Momentum

Chapter 6 – The Moments of Agility in Heterogeneous Teams - More than Events, a True Momentum

In the context of heterogeneous teams, key moments in the agile cycle, such as planning, iterative development, and continuous feedback, play a central role in maintaining consistency, agility, and adaptability. These moments, also known as "events" in Scrum, go beyond mere execution of practices; they become true "momentums" that propel the team toward constant improvement and alignment. In this chapter, we will explore how each moment of the agile cycle can be addressed and adapted by teams with different skills, cultures, and work styles, ensuring cohesion and operational effectiveness.

6.1 The Planning Moment

The Planning Moment represents one of the central aspects of the agile cycle and is crucial for ensuring that the team starts each iteration with clarity and cohesion. In heterogeneous teams, where cultural, linguistic, and geographical differences can influence communication and decision-making, planning requires special attention to maintain alignment among all members.

6.1.1. Active Involvement of All Team Members

In a heterogeneous team, it is essential to ensure that every member actively participates in the planning process. However, cultural and linguistic differences can affect how team members express themselves and contribute to the discussion. In some cultures, for example, there may be a tendency to avoid direct confrontation or not express opposing opinions in a group setting, which can lead to decisions being made without true consensus.

The Product Owner and the facilitator (such as the Scrum Master or another team leader) must create an environment that encourages open dialogue and participation. Techniques such as open-ended questioning or round-robin (where each team member has the opportunity to speak in turn) can help engage everyone fairly. The use of asynchronous collaboration tools can be useful for gathering contributions from team members who may feel less comfortable speaking in real time.

6.1.2. Managing Time Zones and Geographic Distribution

In geographically distributed teams, managing time zones is one of the main challenges during planning. It is essential to find a balance that allows all members to participate in planning meetings without feeling penalized. When it is not possible to find a time that works for everyone, a possible solution is to adopt an asynchronous planning model.

For example, the team could use a project management platform like Jira or Trello to set up a shared board where each member can contribute to planning and prioritization at the most suitable time. This allows everyone to have a voice and ensures that planning is as inclusive as possible, despite logistical difficulties.

6.1.3. Clear Definition of Goals and Priorities

One of the main challenges in planning heterogeneous teams is the clear definition of goals and priorities. Different professional experiences or cultural contexts can influence how team members perceive the importance of certain tasks or features. It is crucial for the Product Owner to communicate the main objectives of the work cycle clearly, using language that is understandable to all team members.

To overcome these differences, it may be useful to adopt a more visual approach to planning, using dashboards or kanban boards to make tasks and their priorities visible to everyone. Additionally, a shared prioritization system, such as the Eisenhower matrix or other prioritization techniques, can help the team reach a consensus on the most important activities.

6.1.4. Adapting the Planning Process to the Framework Used

In heterogeneous teams using different frameworks, such as Scrum or Kanban, the planning process must be adapted based on the chosen methodology. In Scrum, for example, planning occurs at the beginning of each sprint and involves defining a clear sprint goal. In Kanban, however, planning is more fluid, and work is managed on a continuous basis.

In the context of heterogeneous teams, it is important to ensure that the planning process remains flexible. Teams using Scrum can, for example, schedule shorter but more frequent planning moments to avoid overwhelming team members with long meetings. In teams using Kanban, it is possible to plan small checkpoints to regularly verify that the workflow is well managed and that there are no bottlenecks.

6.1.5. Inclusion of Diversity of Experiences and Skills

The strength of a heterogeneous team lies in the diversity of experiences and skills. During planning, it is important to leverage this diversity to gain a broader and more comprehensive view of the work to be done. However, this diversity can also be a challenge, as members with different skills may have different expectations on how to manage certain tasks.

To overcome these differences, it is essential for the team to actively collaborate in defining work strategies. Techniques such as guided brainstorming or planning poker can help stimulate participation and ensure that all viewpoints are considered. It is also important for team members to understand and respect each other's skills, avoiding unnecessary conflicts arising from differences in opinions or work styles.

6.1.6. Conclusion of the Planning Moment

In summary, planning in a heterogeneous team is not just a matter of deciding what to do, but ensuring that all team members have a clear and shared alignment. With open communication, appropriate collaborative tools, and adaptation to specific cultural and geographical needs, the Planning Moment can become an opportunity for the team to strengthen cohesion and create a solid foundation for future work.

6.2 The Iterative Development Moment

The Iterative Development Moment is the beating heart of any agile methodology. In this phase, the team takes the planned tasks and begins to transform them into tangible value through short, iterative development cycles. In heterogeneous teams, where cultural, geographical, and technical skill differences can amplify operational complexities, the effectiveness of iterative development depends on the group's ability to adapt, collaborate, and maintain a continuous and coordinated workflow.

6.2.1. Teamwork and Effective Collaboration

In heterogeneous teams, collaboration is fundamental to overcoming communication and work style barriers. During the iterative development cycle, team members must work closely together, sharing information, solving problems in real time, and ensuring everyone is aligned with the goals.

To facilitate collaboration in teams with diverse skills and backgrounds, it may be helpful to encourage practices like pair programming, where two developers work together on a single task. This not only fosters knowledge sharing but also helps improve code quality by reducing errors and increasing mutual understanding among team members.

In distributed teams, real-time collaboration tools such as GitHub, GitLab, or communication platforms like Slack or

Microsoft Teams can help maintain continuous communication during development. It is crucial that each member has clear visibility into what others are doing to avoid duplicating work or misunderstandings.

6.2.2. Adapting to Team Speed and Capacity

One of the most delicate aspects of iterative development in a heterogeneous team is managing the differences in speed and capacity among group members. Some members may have advanced technical skills and complete tasks more quickly, while others may need more time to tackle similar tasks. This divergence can create imbalances and lead to tensions within the team if not managed properly.

To address this challenge, the team should adopt a culture of mentoring and mutual support. More experienced members can help less experienced ones overcome technical difficulties, while team members with deeper knowledge in specific areas can offer valuable insights to solve complex problems.

Additionally, setting realistic iterative goals for each sprint or work cycle is essential for keeping the team motivated and productive. The Product Owner and Scrum Master must consider individual capabilities and the overall workload of the team, avoiding overloading some members or underutilizing others.

6.2.3. Managing Technical Debt

During iterative development, technical debt is one of the most common challenges teams face. Technical debt accumulates when short-term solutions are preferred over optimal ones to meet deadlines, compromising code quality or architecture. In heterogeneous teams, this situation can be exacerbated by the differing experiences and expectations regarding code quality and development processes.

To manage technical debt, it is essential to implement a rigorous code review strategy and involve all team members in discussions about technical solutions. Source control tools like Git can be used to monitor and improve code quality, ensuring that all team members adhere to the same technical standards.

Another useful practice is to include refactoring activities in the team's backlog, so that technical debt does not accumulate over time. The Product Owner and development team must balance the need for new features with the necessity of addressing technical issues that could slow long-term progress.

6.2.4. Synchronization and Coordination in Distributed Teams

In the iterative development cycle, continuous synchronization is crucial to keep the team aligned with the goals and to address any issues in real time. In distributed teams, where members work in different time zones or on geographically distant sites, synchronization can be a significant challenge.

Daily or weekly stand-up meetings provide an opportunity to check the status of work and identify any obstacles. In heterogeneous teams, it may be necessary to adopt asynchronous stand-up models, where team members record their updates in written or video format, allowing others to consult this information at a more convenient time.

This approach avoids penalizing team members who work in incompatible hours.

Furthermore, continuous integration (CI/CD) pipelines can help synchronize development work more efficiently. Tools like Jenkins, CircleCI, or integrated pipelines in GitLab can automate build, test, and deployment processes, ensuring that the team continuously delivers value and that the code remains consistent across iterations.

6.2.5. Iterative Feedback on Work Progress

Continuous feedback is one of the key elements of the iterative development cycle, allowing teams to quickly course-correct and improve the product step by step. In heterogeneous teams, feedback must be managed carefully, as cultural or linguistic differences can lead to misunderstandings or make it difficult to express constructive criticism.

To enhance the feedback flow, it is helpful to adopt a formal review approach and pair reviews. Each team member should have the opportunity to receive clear and specific feedback on what they are doing well and how they could improve. This process not only helps resolve technical issues but also improves collaboration within the team.

6.2.6. Conclusion of the Iterative Development Moment

In conclusion, the Iterative Development Moment in heterogeneous teams requires greater attention to collaboration, management of capacity differences, and code quality. By adopting collaborative practices like mentoring and pair programming, and carefully managing technical debt and continuous synchronization, teams can overcome barriers and create a productive and iterative workflow. The success of iterative development depends on the team's ability to adapt to differences and maintain a constant focus on long-term goals.

6.3 The Continuous Feedback Moment

Continuous feedback is one of the fundamental pillars of agility, as it allows teams to constantly evaluate their work, course-correct, and improve processes throughout the development cycle. In heterogeneous teams, the Feedback Moment assumes even greater importance, as cultural, linguistic, and operational differences can complicate communication and the ability to effectively give and receive feedback.

To ensure that feedback is constructive and useful in heterogeneous teams, it is necessary to adopt approaches that facilitate clarity, mutual respect, and the inclusion of all members, ensuring that everyone's opinions and contributions are heard and valued.

6.3.1. Creating a Trust and Psychological Safety Environment

In heterogeneous teams, the first challenge in ensuring effective continuous feedback is creating a trust environment. In multicultural contexts, some team members may be reluctant to express criticism or suggestions, fearing that these may be perceived negatively or harm interpersonal relationships.

The team facilitator (such as a Scrum Master or project leader) has the task of promoting a culture of constructive feedback, where all members feel free to express their opinions without fear of repercussions. This can be achieved by encouraging the use of positive, non-judgmental language and promoting practices like fact-based feedback, which relies on objective observations rather than personal evaluations.

6.3.2. Adapting Feedback to Cultural Differences

Cultural differences can significantly influence how feedback is given and received. In some cultures, direct and honest feedback is seen as a sign of professionalism, while in others, a more indirect and diplomatic approach is preferred. In heterogeneous teams, it is crucial to recognize and respect these differences, adapting the communication style based on the context.

For instance, in teams distributed across multiple countries, a more delicate approach might be adopted during retrospective or peer review sessions, emphasizing the team's successes before addressing areas for improvement. Tools like anonymous feedback forms can also help overcome cultural barriers, allowing team members to express their opinions more freely and informally.

6.3.3. Asynchronous Feedback in Distributed Teams

Another challenge in heterogeneous teams, especially those geographically distributed, is managing real-time feedback. In teams spread across different time zones, it can be difficult to organize meetings that involve all members simultaneously. In such cases, asynchronous feedback becomes a valuable resource.

Collaborative platforms like Slack, Microsoft Teams, or Trello can be used to collect feedback asynchronously, allowing team members to provide their opinions and assessments based on their availability. The use of shared documents to track comments and observations can further improve visibility and transparency, ensuring that all members have equal and timely access to feedback.

6.3.4. Feedback as a Tool for Personal and Professional Growth

Feedback in heterogeneous teams should not only focus on improving the product or process but also on the personal and professional growth of individual team members. In heterogeneous environments, where members may have different skills, experiences, and work styles, feedback represents an opportunity to enhance collaboration and strengthen individual competencies.

One useful tool for this purpose is 360-degree feedback, which allows each team member to receive input from peers, supervisors, and subordinates. This approach provides a holistic view of each member's performance, helping to identify not only strengths but also areas for improvement.

6.3.5. Facilitating Open Discussions During Retrospectives

Retrospectives are one of the main moments when the agile team can reflect on successes and obstacles encountered during a development cycle. In heterogeneous teams, facilitating open and productive discussions during retrospectives can be complicated by communication differences and potential cultural conflicts.

The facilitator must therefore adopt an inclusive approach, encouraging all team members to actively participate in discussions and ensuring that no voice is ignored. Tools like digital sticky notes or virtual boards can help gather ideas anonymously, ensuring that even the more reserved members can contribute. Retrospectives should become a moment of sharing and mutual learning, where the team feels free to express constructive criticism and propose improvement solutions.

6.3.6. Conclusion of the Continuous Feedback Moment

In conclusion, the Continuous Feedback Moment in heterogeneous teams requires attention to cultural differences, communication dynamics, and the need to create an environment of trust and mutual respect. Feedback, when managed effectively, can become a powerful tool for improving collaboration and work quality within the team. By adopting practices that promote transparency, respect, and inclusivity, heterogeneous teams can leverage feedback to grow and constantly improve, both individually and collectively.

Chapter 6 – The Moments of Agility in Heterogeneous Teams - More than Events, a True Momentum

6.4 The Review and Improvement Moment

The Review and Improvement Moment, which primarily occurs during sprint reviews and retrospectives, is crucial for evaluating the results of iterations and implementing continuous improvements. In heterogeneous teams, the review goes beyond just the quality of the final product; it also becomes a tool for enhancing collaboration dynamics among members with diverse backgrounds.

6.4.1. Reviewing Iteration Results

During sprint reviews, the team has the opportunity to present the completed work and receive feedback from stakeholders. In heterogeneous teams, cultural diversity and differences in expectations can complicate this process. It is essential that the results are presented in a clear and understandable manner for all, using visual tools and shared metrics to minimize ambiguity.

The team must ensure that every member understands how their contributions fit into the overall project framework. This is particularly important in distributed contexts, where a lack of visibility into other areas of work can create misalignments.

6.4.2. Retrospectives as Opportunities for Improvement

Retrospectives are a fundamental moment for continuous improvement. In heterogeneous teams, retrospectives provide added value, as they allow reflection not only on technical aspects but also on how cultural and operational dynamics influence teamwork. In these contexts, it may be useful to employ structured techniques like the starfish retrospective, which helps the team identify what should be kept, improved, reduced, or started.

The primary goal of the retrospective is to ensure that the team learns from both successes and failures, continuously adapting their work methods. In heterogeneous teams, this process must also include assessing communication and collaboration methods among members, identifying any barriers that might hinder overall effectiveness.

6.4.3. Adapting Practices to Team Needs

Continuous improvement should not be limited to technical solutions; in heterogeneous teams, it is also important to adapt work practices to the specific needs of members. For instance, a distributed team might find that some meetings are too long for everyone's time zones or that certain communication tools are not effective for all members.

Retrospectives should be a space to discuss these aspects and implement concrete changes that enhance the team's efficiency. This includes modifications to work processes, tools used, and the frequency of meetings.

6.4.4. Involving Stakeholders in Sprint Reviews

Another critical aspect for heterogeneous teams is managing stakeholder expectations during sprint reviews. Cultural or geographical differences can influence how stakeholders perceive the team's progress. Ensuring that their expectations are aligned with the team's objectives and capabilities is essential to avoid misunderstandings and maintain trust.

Stakeholders should be actively involved in sprint reviews, where the team can receive direct feedback and adjust their work accordingly. This moment is crucial to ensure that the final product meets the actual needs of the customer, preventing physical distance or communication differences from compromising alignment on expected results.

6.4.5. Conclusion of the Review and Improvement Moment

The Review and Improvement Moment is a valuable opportunity for heterogeneous teams to reflect on their work dynamics and iteration results. In a diverse context, it is essential that this moment is used to promote continuous improvement, not only of technical processes but also of collaboration and communication among members. Through a structured and inclusive approach, heterogeneous teams can continuously enhance their performance and maintain constructive alignment both internally and with stakeholders.

6.5 The Stakeholder Engagement Moment

The Stakeholder Engagement Moment is essential to ensure that the team remains aligned with external expectations and that the results of iterations are evaluated by those who will have a direct impact on the project. In heterogeneous teams, this moment requires special attention as cultural and operational differences can influence how stakeholders interpret the team's progress and provide their feedback.

6.5.1. Creating a Clear and Transparent Communication Channel

In a heterogeneous team context, communication with stakeholders can become complex due to differences in language, time zones, and expectations. It is essential to establish a clear and transparent communication channel that ensures stakeholders are regularly and structured informed about the project's progress.

To avoid misunderstandings, the team should utilize tools such as visual dashboards or automated reports that make the team's progress and priorities easily accessible to all stakeholders. These tools should be designed to be understandable even to those without specific technical expertise, ensuring that everyone can correctly interpret the data.

6.5.2. Adapting Engagement to Stakeholder Needs and Styles

Each stakeholder has a different level of engagement and expectations. In heterogeneous teams, where stakeholders may come from diverse cultural backgrounds, it is crucial to adapt communication methods according to their preferences. Some stakeholders may prefer more frequent and detailed updates, while others may be more interested in an overall view of long-term progress.

The team must be able to modulate its interactions, maintaining transparency without overwhelming stakeholders with unnecessary information. The key is to find a balance between providing operational details and keeping the focus on the project's strategic objectives.

6.5.3. Aligning Expectations with Team Reality

One of the biggest challenges in heterogeneous teams is ensuring that stakeholder expectations are realistic compared to the team's capabilities. Cultural and operational differences can lead to misunderstandings about what is technically feasible or how work is progressing. Therefore, it is essential for the team to use the Engagement Moment to clarify its capabilities, limitations, and progress in a realistic and transparent manner.

Sprint reviews provide the opportunity to openly discuss any difficulties encountered with stakeholders and to negotiate changes to objectives or deadlines based on the team's actual capacities. This honest dialogue helps to avoid disappointments and maintains a good relationship between the team and stakeholders.

6.5.4. Receiving Continuous Feedback from Stakeholders

Stakeholder feedback is crucial to ensure that the team is heading in the right direction. In heterogeneous teams, feedback should be received in a regular and structured manner, considering the different cultural and operational perspectives of stakeholders. It is important that feedback is specific, clear, and results-oriented so that the team can adapt its work effectively.

Using feedback collection tools, such as questionnaires or surveys, can facilitate the process in distributed teams and help ensure that stakeholders have a platform to provide their opinions even when they cannot directly participate in review meetings.

6.5.5. Conclusion of the Stakeholder Engagement Moment

In the context of heterogeneous teams, the Stakeholder Engagement Moment is crucial for maintaining continuous alignment with the external objectives of the project. Ensuring that communication is clear, transparent, and tailored to the cultural and operational needs of stakeholders allows the team to avoid misunderstandings and maintain stakeholders' trust over the long term. With active engagement and regular feedback, heterogeneous teams can ensure they stay on the right path and consistently meet stakeholder expectations in a coherent and strategic manner.

Chapter 6 – The Moments of Agility in Heterogeneous Teams - More than Events, a True Momentum

6.6. Momentum of Agile Events in Heterogeneous Teams - Conclusion

The Momentum of Agile Events in heterogeneous teams represents a series of strategic opportunities that go beyond merely organizing meetings or reviews. These moments serve as critical reference points to ensure that the team remains aligned, agile, and ready to tackle the complexities that arise in daily work. In heterogeneous teams, where diversity in skills, cultural backgrounds, and time zones presents a constant challenge, the effectiveness of these events depends on the ability to adapt each phase of the agile cycle to the specificities of the group.

6.6.1. Integrating Agility with Diversity

In heterogeneous teams, agility must be experienced as an approach that transcends standard processes, adapting to internal diversities. Success hinges on the team's ability to leverage the plurality of ideas and approaches, balancing collaboration with effective management of time and resources. Planning meetings, iterative development, continuous feedback, and stakeholder engagement must be continuously refined and improved.

6.6.2. Momentum as a Tool for Cohesion and Growth

Agile "momentum" is not isolated events but powerful tools for keeping the team cohesive and focused on long-term goals. In heterogeneous teams, these moments can become valuable opportunities to facilitate communication, resolve conflicts, and build a sense of mutual trust. Through effective management of these events, teams can overcome cultural and operational barriers, enhancing their ability to respond to changes swiftly and accurately.

6.6.3. Continuous Adaptation and Iterative Improvement

The principle of continuous adaptation should guide every agile team, but in heterogeneous teams, this aspect becomes even more critical. The key to success is constant reflection on processes and internal team dynamics, implementing improvements that not only resolve technical issues but also promote an inclusive and collaborative work environment.

6.6.4. Final Conclusion

In conclusion, the effectiveness of agile momentum in heterogeneous teams depends on the group's ability to adapt, collaborate, and learn continuously. These events are not just opportunities to assess project progress but also to strengthen team cohesion, improve communication, and maintain alignment with business objectives. When managed effectively, agile momentum can become a powerful tool for growth and success for teams operating in complex and diverse contexts.

Chapter 7

Gestione del Cambiamento nei Team Eterogenei

Chapter 7 - Change Management in Heterogeneous Teams

Chapter 7 - Change Management in Heterogeneous Teams

Change is a constant in modern organizations, but in heterogeneous teams, change management requires an even more careful and structured approach. Cultural, operational, and skill differences can complicate the process of adopting new practices, methodologies, or tools. In this chapter, we will explore how teams can effectively face and manage change, ensuring that all members are aligned and motivated to collaborate towards common goals.

7.1 Preparing the Team for Change

Preparing the team is one of the fundamental elements for ensuring a smooth transition during the implementation of change. In heterogeneous teams, this phase becomes even more crucial, as cultural, operational, and background differences can influence how members perceive and react to change.

7.1.1. Clearly Communicate Objectives and Benefits

The first step in preparation is to ensure that all team members clearly understand the objectives of the change and the benefits that will arise. In heterogeneous teams, where language or cultural barriers may hinder understanding, it is essential to provide clear and structured communication.

Team leaders must explain not only what will change but also why this change is necessary. Tools like visual presentations, infographics, or explanatory videos can be utilized to make the message more accessible to everyone. Furthermore, it is beneficial to highlight how the change will benefit the team as a whole and individual members, both professionally and operationally.

7.1.2. Tailor the Message to Cultural Differences

In a heterogeneous team, reactions to change can vary based on cultural differences. Some members may come from backgrounds where change is viewed as a threat or challenge, while others may see it as an opportunity for growth and innovation.

To overcome these differences, leaders must tailor the message to the diverse cultural sensitivities within the team. For example, in cultures that highly respect authority, it may be more effective for changes to be communicated by executives or project heads. In more collaborative cultures, it might be beneficial to involve the team more in the decision-making process, encouraging dialogue and active participation from the outset.

7.1.3. Provide Support and Training Tools

To ensure that the change is successfully implemented, it is essential to provide the team with the necessary training tools. This is particularly important in heterogeneous teams, where levels of expertise and familiarity with new practices or tools can vary widely.

Offering workshops, interactive tutorials, and mentoring sessions can help team members feel more confident and prepared. Additionally, support should be ongoing: it is important to create support channels where members can ask questions or seek clarification even during the transition phase.

7.1.4. Create an Active Listening Environment

Preparing for change involves not only giving instructions but also actively listening to the concerns, suggestions, and resistance of the team. In a heterogeneous team, this aspect is especially important, as members may have different opinions about the change based on their past experiences and expectations.

Leaders must promote an active listening environment, where every team member feels free to express their views. Tools like anonymous surveys or open feedback sessions can be used to gather valuable input and identify critical areas that may require greater attention. This approach not only helps mitigate resistance but also ensures that the change is perceived as a shared and collaborative process.

7.1.5. Conclusion of Preparation

In summary, preparing a heterogeneous team for change requires a structured, flexible, and inclusive approach. Clearly communicating objectives, adapting the message to cultural differences, providing support, and creating an active listening environment are essential steps to ensure that every team member feels involved and ready to face the transition. With proper preparation, the team can proactively approach change, viewing it as an opportunity for growth rather than a challenge.

7.2. Active Involvement of All Team Members

Active involvement of all team members is an essential component for the success of any change initiative. In heterogeneous teams, this aspect takes on even greater importance, as cultural, operational, and skill differences can influence how members engage in the process. To ensure that change is successfully adopted, it is necessary to create inclusive participation opportunities where every team member can express themselves and contribute.

7.2.1. Create Opportunities for Active Participation

In a heterogeneous team, some members may be less inclined to actively participate in change processes, especially in contexts where open communication is not a common practice. To overcome this barrier, it is important to create spaces where every team member feels free to participate without pressure.

Tools such as interactive workshops, brainstorming sessions, or focus groups can encourage dialogue and the sharing of ideas. Additionally, using digital collaboration platforms, such as Slack or Trello, can facilitate participation from all members, especially in geographically distributed teams, allowing members to contribute asynchronously without being constrained by time zone or language barriers.

7.2.2. Encourage Diversity of Opinions

In heterogeneous teams, it is essential to value the diversity of opinions. Team members come from different backgrounds and may have unique perspectives on change. Encouraging debate and the expression of differing ideas not only enriches the decision-making process but also increases the level of involvement.

To achieve this, the team facilitator must promote an environment of mutual respect and openness, where opposing opinions are not ignored or marginalized. Techniques such as guided brainstorming or round-robin discussions, where everyone has the opportunity to speak, can help ensure that every member has a voice and prevent only dominant opinions from prevailing.

7.2.3. Engage Members with Different Skill Levels

In a heterogeneous team, not all members have the same level of experience or technical competence. It is important that active involvement takes these differences into account, ensuring that even less experienced members have the opportunity to contribute and grow within the team.

Tools such as mentoring and pair programming can be utilized to facilitate skill exchange among team members. This approach not only promotes continuous learning but also fosters a collaborative work environment where team members support each other during the change process.

7.2.4. Remove Communication Barriers

Communication barriers can pose a significant obstacle to active participation in heterogeneous teams. Linguistic or cultural differences can influence how team members understand and respond to information related to change. To address this challenge, it is essential to use clear communication tailored to the needs of all members.

The team should adopt simplified communication, avoiding overly technical terminology or unfamiliar acronyms. Utilizing visual aids such as infographics, diagrams, or concept maps can help ensure that messages are clear and comprehensible to everyone, regardless of their language proficiency.

7.2.5. Promote Asynchronous Collaboration

In distributed teams, active involvement may be limited by time zone differences or personal commitments. To overcome this obstacle, it is important to promote asynchronous collaboration, allowing team members to participate in change processes according to their availability.

Asynchronous collaboration tools, such as Trello, Confluence, or Google Docs, enable team members to contribute to discussions and express their ideas without having to attend real-time meetings. This approach ensures that all members have the opportunity to participate equally, even if they cannot be physically or virtually present at specific times.

7.2.6. Conclusion on Active Involvement

The active involvement of all team members is essential to ensure that change is accepted and implemented successfully. In heterogeneous teams, this requires additional effort to create inclusive participation opportunities, value diverse opinions, support members with varying skills, and remove communication barriers. Through effective participation management, the team can collaboratively approach change, ensuring that all members feel like integral parts of the transformation process.

7.3. Overcoming Resistance to Change

Resistance to change is a common phenomenon in any organization, but in heterogeneous teams, it can take on more complex forms due to cultural, operational, and personal differences. Resistance can arise from various factors, including uncertainty about the future, fear of losing control, or a lack of trust in the change itself. To manage and overcome this resistance, it is necessary to adopt an empathetic and strategic approach that recognizes and proactively addresses the team's concerns.

7.3.1 Recognizing and Understanding the Causes of Resistance

The first step in overcoming resistance to change is recognizing and understanding its causes. In heterogeneous teams, resistance can stem from multiple sources: cultural differences, negative past experiences, or simply the difficulty of adapting to new operating methods. In some cases, team members may perceive change as a threat to their job stability or as an imposition from above without a clear benefit.

To address these concerns, it is essential to conduct open conversations with team members. Leaders should actively listen and show understanding of the difficulties and fears expressed, fostering a dialogue that demonstrates a commitment to solving issues. Tools like individual listening sessions or focus groups can help surface these concerns constructively.

7.3.2 Demonstrating the Benefits of Change

An effective way to overcome resistance is to clearly showcase the benefits of the change. Often, resistance arises because team members do not see how the change can improve their situation or how they work. In heterogeneous teams, it is important to explain the advantages not only at the organizational level but also on a personal level, such as improving collaboration, increasing skills, or reducing inefficiencies.

Using concrete examples, such as case studies of teams that have successfully undergone similar changes, can help team members understand the added value of the change. It is also useful to highlight short-term benefits to alleviate anxiety about transformations that may seem too large or distant.

7.3.3 Promoting Involvement in Defining the Change

Resistance often diminishes when team members feel involved in the change process. In heterogeneous teams, it is crucial to offer opportunities for active participation in defining how the change will be implemented. This not only fosters a sense of belonging but also allows for the integration of diverse perspectives and cultural sensitivities into the process.

Tools like co-creation sessions or design thinking workshops can be effective in engaging the team in change planning, enabling them to contribute ideas and practical solutions. This approach promotes a sense of shared responsibility and reduces the perception of change as a top-down decision.

7.3.4 Offering Continuous Training and Support

The fear of being unable to cope with change is another common source of resistance, especially in heterogeneous teams, where levels of competence and familiarity with new practices can vary widely. To mitigate this fear, it is essential to provide the necessary training and ongoing support.

Targeted training sessions, coaching, and mentoring can help team members feel more confident in mastering the new skills required. Support should not be limited to an initial phase but should be available throughout the entire transition process. Utilizing e-learning platforms or collaborative learning tools can facilitate access to training, ensuring that every team member can progress at their own pace.

7.3.5 Providing a Positive Example through Leadership

Leadership plays a crucial role in overcoming resistance to change. Team leaders must act as positive role models, demonstrating commitment and confidence in the change. In heterogeneous teams, it is particularly important for leaders to show empathy and understanding towards the diverse experiences and concerns of the group.

A leader who is visibly engaged in the change and open to dialogue creates a trusting environment. Organizing regular check-ins to monitor how the team is managing the change and providing support during difficult times can be an effective way to reduce resistance and promote a positive attitude.

7.3.6 Conclusion on Overcoming Resistance

Overcoming resistance to change in heterogeneous teams requires a strategic approach that integrates understanding, effective communication, and ongoing support. Recognizing concerns, actively involving team members, and providing training are essential steps in creating an environment where change is not seen as a threat but as an opportunity. With strong leadership and constant dialogue, resistance can be transformed into a driving force for the team's success during the transition.

7.4. Adapting Change to Teams Dynamics

Every team has its own dynamics, shaped by the competencies, personalities, cultures, and working styles of its members. In heterogeneous teams, where these differences are often more pronounced, it is essential that the change process is adapted to meet the specific needs and characteristics of the group. Implementing change based on rigid, standardized models without considering internal diversities can lead to resistance and misunderstandings. Therefore, adapting change to the team dynamics is crucial for ensuring the success of the transformation.

7.4.1 Recognizing and Valuing Cultural Differences

In heterogeneous teams, cultural differences play a significant role in how members perceive and manage change. Some may come from backgrounds where change is viewed with enthusiasm, while others might have a more conservative outlook. It is essential that the change is adapted with these sensitivities in mind.

The first step is to recognize and value the cultural differences within the team. Organizing intercultural awareness meetings or workshops can help members better understand their colleagues' backgrounds, facilitating communication and collaboration during the change process. Additionally, leaders must adopt a flexible approach, modulating the change process to respect and integrate different cultural perspectives.

7.4.2 Customizing the Approach Based on Competencies

Competencies can vary significantly in heterogeneous teams, and a change approach that does not account for these differences risks creating imbalances and frustrations. To avoid this, the change process must be customized according to the technical and operational competencies of individual team members.

For example, in teams where some members are more experienced with new technologies or agile practices while others have a more traditional background, it may be beneficial to implement a mentoring or peer collaboration system, where more experienced members help less knowledgeable ones master new practices. Additionally, the pace of change must be adapted to ensure that all team members have time to learn and adapt without feeling overwhelmed.

7.4.3 Managing Differences in Working Styles

In heterogeneous teams, differences in working styles can emerge strongly during change. Some members may be action-oriented, preferring a rapid, hands-on approach, while others may favor a period of reflection and analysis before implementing new solutions. It is important for leaders to recognize these differences and adapt the change process so that no team member feels alienated.

An effective way to manage differences in working styles is to create intermediate phases in the change process, where the team can reflect on progress made and make adjustments to the approach. This allows both action-oriented members and those who are more reflective to find a balance between rapid implementation and careful analysis.

7.4.4 Flexibility in the Change Process

Flexibility is a crucial component in adapting change to team dynamics. A rigid approach may not work in heterogeneous teams, where conditions and needs can vary significantly. Adopting an iterative change process that allows the team to make modifications and adjustments along the way can help ensure that all members are involved and comfortable.

To promote this flexibility, leaders should implement a checkpoint-based approach, where the team can discuss difficulties encountered, successes achieved, and any modifications needed in the process. Tools like retrospectives or focus groups can facilitate these discussions, allowing the team to adapt flexibly to new challenges.

7.4.5 Monitoring the Impact of Change on Team Dynamics

Another important aspect of adapting change is continuously monitoring its impact on team dynamics. In heterogeneous teams, where interactions and collaboration can be influenced by multiple factors, it is essential for leaders to keep track of how the change is affecting relationships between team members and their productivity.

Using internal assessment tools or anonymous surveys can provide valuable insights into how team members are experiencing the change and any issues that may arise. This monitoring should be ongoing and proactive, allowing for timely interventions if difficulties or tensions emerge within the group.

7.4.6 Conclusion on Adapting Change

Adapting change to the dynamics of a heterogeneous team requires a flexible and personalized approach. Recognizing cultural differences, managing diversity in competencies and working styles, and continuously monitoring the impact of change are fundamental elements for ensuring a successful transition. With an iterative and dialogue-oriented process, leaders can ensure that every team member feels involved and supported during the transformation, fostering greater cohesion and collaboration.

7.5. Monitoring Progress and Impact of Change

Continuous monitoring of the progress and impact of change is crucial to ensure that the transformation process is effective and well-managed. In heterogeneous teams, where there are significant differences in skills, working styles, and cultural backgrounds, monitoring becomes even more important. Not only does it allow for the evaluation of technical progress, but it also helps in understanding how the change impacts team dynamics and collaboration among members. Regular monitoring enables leaders to identify issues in real-time, make corrections, and ensure that the change aligns with the overall objectives.

7.5.1 Define Clear and Measurable Indicators

Before monitoring change progress, it is essential to establish clear and measurable indicators (KPIs) that can serve as evaluation parameters. In heterogeneous teams, these indicators should be tailored to the specifics of the team and the project. For example, one KPI might focus on the team's ability to adopt new technologies, while another might assess improvement in collaboration among members with diverse skills.

The progress indicators must be realistic and well-understood by all team members. Clearly communicating what the success parameters are allows everyone to have a clear vision of what they are trying to achieve, creating common alignment and focus.

7.5.2 Utilize Continuous Monitoring Tools

To ensure that monitoring is efficient, it is important to use continuous monitoring tools that allow for real-time data collection and constant evaluation of change progress. In heterogeneous teams, where work may be distributed geographically and operational modes may vary, digital tools such as performance dashboards, automated reports, and project management software are essential.

Tools like Jira, Trello, or Asana can be configured to provide a detailed view of how the team is handling new practices and the effectiveness of the change. These tools help monitor timelines, completed activities, delays, and technical difficulties, allowing leaders to intervene quickly where necessary.

7.5.3 Evaluate Impact on Team Dynamics

In addition to technical progress, it is important to monitor the impact of change on group dynamics. In heterogeneous teams, interpersonal relationships and collaboration among members can be affected by the change in ways that may not immediately surface. For example, the adoption of new practices might create tensions among members with different working approaches or lead to a decrease in motivation for those struggling to keep up.

To assess these aspects, it may be useful to conduct anonymous surveys or regular feedback sessions where team members can express their concerns or highlight difficulties in internal dynamics. This feedback allows leaders to identify latent problems and take corrective actions to improve the work environment and maintain team cohesion during the transition.

7.5.4 Adopt an Iterative Approach

The monitoring process in heterogeneous teams should be iterative, meaning it should involve continuous adjustments based on the results obtained. Rather than evaluating the change only at the end of the process, it is important to establish regular checkpoints where the team can reflect on the progress made and any modifications needed.

Retrospectives are an excellent tool for implementing this iterative approach. After each work cycle or sprint, the team can discuss what worked and what can be improved. This process not only allows for correcting any mistakes along the way but also strengthens team cohesion, as all members actively participate in improving the process.

7.5.5 Correcting Course Where Necessary

One of the primary objectives of continuous monitoring is to be able to correct course quickly if the change is not yielding the desired results or if unforeseen problems arise. In heterogeneous teams, this ability to adjust is particularly important, as cultural and operational differences can bring unexpected obstacles to the change process.

When problems are detected, leaders must be ready to intervene quickly, making adjustments to the initial plan without compromising the consistency of the approach. This could mean providing additional training support, revising change objectives, or adapting collaboration methods to better meet the team's needs.

7.5.6 Conclusion on Monitoring Progress

Continuous monitoring of progress and the impact of change is essential for ensuring the success of the transformation in heterogeneous teams. Defining clear indicators, using effective monitoring tools, evaluating the impact on team dynamics, and adopting an iterative approach allow for effective oversight of the change and timely adjustments. With careful and proactive monitoring, teams can navigate change more effectively, reducing risks and maximizing the benefits of the transformation process.

7.6. Strengthening Team Cohesion During Change

During change processes, maintaining and strengthening team cohesion is crucial for the success of the transformation. In heterogeneous teams, where cultural, technical, and skill differences are more pronounced, the risk that change may cause misalignments or tensions is elevated. Therefore, it is essential to adopt measures that not only effectively manage the change but also reinforce the bonds within the team and promote collaboration.

7.6.1 Create a Trusting and Supportive Environment

Trust is the foundation of cohesion in any team, and it is even more critical in heterogeneous teams. During change, it is essential that team members feel supported and secure, knowing they can express their concerns without fear of repercussions.

To build this environment, leaders must adopt an empathetic and open approach, demonstrating genuine interest in the well-being of team members. Organizing regular meetings to discuss not only technical progress but also internal dynamics can help consolidate trust among members and ensure that everyone feels integral to the change process.

7.6.2 Promote Active Collaboration

Active collaboration is one of the most effective tools for strengthening team cohesion during change. In heterogeneous teams, where there may be cultural or linguistic barriers, it is essential to encourage frequent and constructive interactions among team members.

Techniques such as pair programming, cross-mentoring, or cross-functional working groups can foster the exchange of skills and knowledge among team members, improving mutual understanding and reducing divisions. These tools not only facilitate technical problem-solving but also help team members feel more connected and build stronger relationships.

7.6.3 Celebrate Successes and Small Milestones

During change processes, it is easy for the team to focus solely on challenges and difficulties, neglecting the successes achieved. In heterogeneous teams, celebrating small milestones and recognizing progress is fundamental to maintaining morale and strengthening cohesion.

Leaders should organize regular moments to acknowledge team achievements, even if they are small successes. This could include thank-you meetings or brief ceremonies to celebrate the completion of a critical phase of change. These moments help team members feel appreciated and recognize the value of their contribution to the overall process.

7.6.4 Foster Integration Among Diverse Skills

One of the main advantages of heterogeneous teams is the diversity of skills and perspectives. During change, it is essential to leverage this diversity to create an environment of learning and innovation. Promoting the integration of skills within the team can strengthen cohesion, allowing members to learn from each other and collaborate more effectively.

Encouraging the creation of interdisciplinary working groups or organizing skill-sharing sessions can facilitate this integration. This way, team members not only collaborate more closely but also learn new skills and approaches that can be beneficial for the success of the change and for future projects.

7.6.5 Manage Conflicts Constructively

Change can generate tensions and conflicts, especially in heterogeneous teams, where differences in approach and vision are more pronounced. It is crucial for leaders to be prepared to manage conflicts constructively, transforming them into opportunities for growth and improvement.

Adopting a proactive approach to conflict management, through techniques such as mediation or the use of external facilitators, can help resolve tensions before they become detrimental to team cohesion. Leaders should also create a safe space where members can openly express their opinions, fostering dialogue and mutual understanding.

7.6.6 Conclusion on Strengthening Cohesion

Strengthening team cohesion during change is fundamental to ensuring that the process is successful. In heterogeneous teams, where cultural, operational, and skill differences can amplify difficulties, promoting trust, active collaboration, and recognition of successes is essential for maintaining balance and harmony within the group. With an empathetic and inclusive approach, leaders can transform change into an opportunity to consolidate team cohesion and create a stronger, more collaborative work environment.

7.7. Conclusion of the Chapter: Adapting Change to Heterogeneous Teams

Managing change in a heterogeneous team requires a more flexible and personalized approach compared to a more homogeneous one. The cultural, technical, and operational differences within the team present both challenges and opportunities. The success of the change largely depends on the leaders' ability to adapt to the specific needs of the group and to address complexities with targeted and inclusive strategies.

7.7.1 Summary of Key Success Factors

In managing change in heterogeneous teams, several key factors have been highlighted that can make the difference between a successful transition and a challenging experience. These include:

• Thorough preparation of the team, with clear communication of the objectives and benefits of the change.
• Active involvement of all members, respecting and valuing cultural and skill differences.
• The ability to overcome resistance, providing support, training, and opportunities for participation.
• Constant attention to adapting team dynamics, ensuring that the change process aligns with diverse working styles.

- Continuous monitoring of progress, utilizing appropriate tools and the ability to make timely adjustments.
- Building cohesion by enhancing collaboration and celebrating team successes throughout the change journey.

7.7.2 Building a Culture of Continuous Change

In the long term, heterogeneous teams that embrace change as a natural part of their operation tend to be more resilient and capable of facing new challenges. Rather than viewing change as an extraordinary event, these teams learn to live change as an ongoing culture, where adaptation and innovation become daily practices.

Building a culture of continuous improvement means developing a collective mindset that values feedback, iterative improvement, and constant learning. For leaders, this entails the necessity of keeping communication channels open and creating spaces where the team can reflect on their progress, explore new ideas, and tackle future challenges.

7.7.3 General Conclusion of the Chapter

In conclusion, addressing change in heterogeneous teams is not a simple task, but it is a process that, when managed carefully, can lead to significant benefits. Teams that manage to overcome the challenges of change emerge more cohesive, innovative, and capable of handling greater complexities. By adopting flexible approaches, actively involving all members, and empathetically managing internal dynamics, teams can not only successfully navigate change but also transform it into a driver for growth and continuous improvement.

Chapter 8

Continuous Adaptation and Review in Heterogeneous Teams

Chapter 8 - Continuous Adaptation and Review in Heterogeneous Teams

Chapter 8 - Continuous Adaptation and Review in Heterogeneous Teams

In heterogeneous teams, continuous adaptation and regular review of priorities and backlogs are essential to maintain efficiency and respond to the dynamic needs of a project. Due to the diverse skills, cultural backgrounds, and work approaches, these teams must be able to quickly adapt to changes while balancing the need for flexibility with a solid structure that enables effective planning. In this chapter, we will explore how teams tackle these crucial moments, and we will also analyze a case study from research and development in a large manufacturing company to illustrate how the adaptation process was successfully managed.

8.1 Strategic Inclusion in the Prioritization Decision-Making Process

The continuous review process represents one of the fundamental pillars of agile methodologies, allowing teams to adapt quickly to project needs and redefine priorities based on emerging information. In heterogeneous teams, where different skills and cultural backgrounds influence work methods and decision-making, this review becomes even more critical to ensure that all members are aligned and that work proceeds smoothly.

Chapter 8 - Continuous Adaptation and Review in Heterogeneous Teams

8.1.1 Inclusion in Prioritization Decisions

In heterogeneous teams, one of the main risks is that only certain voices prevail in the decision-making process, to the detriment of other equally valid perspectives. To avoid this, it is essential to adopt an inclusive approach to the review of priorities, so that every team member can contribute based on their skills and experience.

Inclusion is not just about allowing everyone to express themselves; it's also about creating an environment where every opinion is considered with appropriate weight. This is particularly important in teams where certain technical skills may be perceived as more relevant than others. Tools like backlog refinement meetings and shared planning sessions can help ensure that all voices are heard and that decisions are made more equitably.

Backlog refinement meetings are valuable opportunities to review priorities together as a team. In these meetings, all members have the chance to discuss their views on what the most urgent or important tasks are. To facilitate the process in heterogeneous teams, using visual tools like kanban boards or mind maps can make discussions more accessible and comprehensible, regardless of the technical skill level of team members.

8.1.2 Balancing Flexibility and Stability

Another challenge in heterogeneous teams is finding the right balance between flexibility and stability. Agility promotes the ability to quickly adapt to changes, but in teams with diverse skills and expectations, too much flexibility can create confusion and uncertainty. Therefore, it is crucial to establish well-defined time windows during which the review of the backlog and priorities can occur.

For example, teams can schedule reviews every two weeks, limiting sudden changes outside these intervals unless there are emergency situations. This ensures that the team maintains a clear direction during each work cycle without being constantly distracted by ongoing modifications. At the same time, it leaves room to address urgent requests when necessary while still maintaining a degree of stability.

In heterogeneous teams, where dynamics can be more complex, a structured approach like this helps maintain focus on project objectives, reducing anxiety associated with constant changes. Stability at key moments provides security for team members, who know they can rely on reliable planning.

8.1.3 Conclusion of the Continuous Review Process

In summary, the continuous review of priorities in heterogeneous teams requires a more inclusive and balanced approach compared to more homogeneous teams. Actively involving all team members in the decision-making process and establishing well-defined review windows are fundamental practices to ensure that the team maintains alignment and that decisions are made considering diverse perspectives. If managed correctly, this process helps the team remain flexible and responsive while providing the necessary stability to achieve project goals.

8.2. Managing Priority Changes in Multidisciplinary Teams

In multidisciplinary teams, where members possess technical, creative, and strategic skills, managing changes in priorities can become a significant challenge. Differences in perspectives and work approaches can generate conflicts, especially when some disciplines perceive their needs as more urgent or crucial than others. Therefore, it is essential to adopt tools and practices that facilitate dialogue and help balance diverse priorities without compromising team alignment.

8.2.1 Facilitating Dialogue Among Different Disciplines

In a heterogeneous team, where experts from various backgrounds—such as engineers, designers, marketing leads, and other profiles—are present, it is essential to create a space for constructive dialogue that allows all voices to be heard. Often, members of a particular discipline tend to prioritize their own needs, which can lead to a distorted view of the project's actual requirements.

To facilitate this process, adopting a shared facilitation model can be extremely beneficial. In this approach, a neutral facilitator guides planning and prioritization review meetings, ensuring that each discipline has space to present its needs and the rationale behind specific requests. This method not only promotes more open communication but also helps reduce conflicts, as decisions are made based on informed discussions rather than impositions from a single party.

An experienced facilitator can mediate between team members, posing key questions that highlight the implications of each change in priority. For example, an engineer might point out the technical implications of accelerating the release of a feature, while marketing might emphasize the commercial urgency of that release. Through this mediation, the team can reach a consensus that takes into account various needs.

8.2.2 The Importance of Metrics for Prioritization

In multidisciplinary teams, where opinions can diverge widely, the use of clear and objective metrics to assess priorities becomes fundamental. Establishing evaluation criteria based on concrete data helps avoid subjective discussions and facilitates more balanced decision-making. Metrics allow quantifying the impact of each activity and making decisions based on information shared by the entire team.

An effective approach is to use tools like the MoSCoW method (Must have, Should have, Could have, Won't have), which helps categorize activities based on their importance and urgency. This method allows the team to identify which tasks must be completed for the project's success and which can be postponed or eliminated, fostering a more pragmatic discussion grounded in real data.

For instance, during a backlog refinement meeting, the team might use metrics such as customer impact, technical complexity, or economic return to determine which tasks should take priority. Each discipline may have a different view of the importance of an activity, but using shared metrics helps create a more comprehensive and objective picture.

8.2.3 Conclusion on Managing Priorities in Multidisciplinary Teams

Managing changes in priorities in multidisciplinary teams requires a structured approach that facilitates dialogue and uses objective metrics to avoid conflicts. Through effective facilitation and the use of clear evaluation criteria, it is possible to balance the needs of different disciplines and ensure that decisions are made equitably and informatively. This process allows the team to maintain alignment and prevents any single discipline from overly influencing the project's direction, fostering a more harmonious and productive collaboration.

8.3. Case Study: R&D in a Large Manufacturing Company

One of the most fitting examples of how a heterogeneous team can effectively address and manage change and continuous review of priorities comes from the research and development (R&D) sector of a large manufacturing company. In this case, the team was composed of members from different departments, each with diverse skills and perspectives: engineers, production experts, and marketing professionals, each contributing their own viewpoint on project priorities.

The initial challenges faced by this team highlight the difficulties that heterogeneous teams encounter when managing change and establishing common priorities. However, by adopting an iterative approach and facilitation practices, the team was able to overcome these challenges and create a cohesive and results-oriented work environment.

8.3.1 Initial Challenges: Divergences in Priorities

In this multidisciplinary team, the initial challenges revolved around strong divergences in priorities. Engineers, focused on the technical aspects of production, believed that time should be dedicated to development and solving project challenges. Conversely, marketing and production leads pushed for accelerating time-to-market, requesting that efforts be concentrated on releasing the product as quickly as possible to respond to commercial and competitive pressures.

These initial divergences led to internal conflicts, slowdowns in decision-making processes, and difficulties in reaching a consensus on which activities were most urgent to address. Each group tended to give more weight to its own needs, overlooking the perspectives and limitations of others. This created a situation where decisions were often postponed, compromising project progress.

8.3.2 Solution: Iterative Facilitation and Backlog Review

To overcome these difficulties, the team decided to adopt an iterative facilitation approach for backlog refinement and planning meetings. In particular, every two weeks, a sprint review was held, during which each discipline had a dedicated space to present its priorities and discuss the technical or commercial implications of the decisions to be made.

This iterative review not only provided everyone with the opportunity to be heard but also allowed for more objective prioritization assessments using shared metrics that all team members could understand and accept. In this context, metrics such as potential commercial impact, technical impact, and associated costs were employed to justify choices transparently and rationally.

Thanks to this structure, the team was able to reduce internal tensions and create a more collaborative environment. Decisions were no longer perceived as the result of unilateral impositions but as outcomes of open and balanced discussions. This iterative approach also allowed the team to make smooth adjustments to the work plan, responding quickly to new information or changes in context without compromising project stability.

8.3.3 Results and Benefits of the Iterative Process

The adoption of an iterative facilitation approach and continuous prioritization review brought numerous benefits to the team and the project. First and foremost, it improved consistency and alignment among the different team members, reducing conflicts and fostering constructive dialogue among engineers, marketing experts, and production leads.

Secondly, the team gained greater flexibility in project management, allowing them to respond promptly to market changes or technical challenges without creating uncertainty or overwhelming team members. Transparency in the decision-making process enhanced trust between various departments, enabling each member to better understand the needs of others.

Finally, the project achieved its time-to-market goals without compromising product quality, demonstrating how a heterogeneous team, with diverse yet complementary approaches, can find innovative solutions and achieve superior results compared to more homogeneous teams.

8.3.4 Conclusion of the Case Study

The case study of R&D in a large manufacturing company clearly demonstrates how managing priorities in a heterogeneous team can be complex, yet highly effective when approached with the right strategies. Through the adoption of iterative facilitation practices and the use of shared metrics, the team was able to overcome initial divergences and create a collaborative environment where decisions were made in an informed and balanced manner. This approach not only improved decision-making but also strengthened team cohesion and its ability to adapt quickly to changes, ensuring project success.

8.4. Adaptation and Priorization in Heterogeneous Teams

Continuous adaptation is a fundamental element for the success of heterogeneous teams. The ability to react quickly to external and internal changes requires a level of proactivity that allows teams not only to passively respond to situations but also to anticipate and manage them effectively. In heterogeneous teams, where differences in skills and cultural backgrounds can be both a resource and a challenge, developing a culture of proactive adaptation is essential for maintaining efficiency and alignment.

8.4.1 Creating a Culture of Continuous Adaptation

To ensure that heterogeneous teams remain flexible and capable of quickly adapting to new needs, it is important to develop a culture of continuous adaptation. This culture promotes the ability to confront change naturally, without it being perceived as a threat or disruption. In heterogeneous teams, the diversity of experiences can be leveraged as a strength to approach changes from different perspectives and develop more creative solutions.

One way to foster this culture is by promoting continuous feedback. Creating regular feedback mechanisms, such as frequent retrospectives or quick check-ins, allows team members to openly discuss the difficulties encountered and opportunities for improvement. This process not only helps resolve immediate issues but also fosters greater trust and transparency among team members, making change a shared and collaborative experience.

8.4.2 Anticipating Challenges and Preparing to Manage Them

In heterogeneous teams, where cultural and operational differences can lead to varying interpretations of priorities and working methods, it is essential to anticipate challenges and prepare to manage them proactively. Proactivity involves the ability to identify potential obstacles before they become real problems and to strategically plan responses.

A useful approach is to conduct periodic risk assessments that involve all team members. These assessments allow for the identification of potentially problematic areas and the development of contingency plans. For example, if a project requires the integration of new technologies, the team can anticipate the difficulties that less experienced members may face and plan training and support activities to mitigate the risk of slowdowns.

8.4.3 Fostering Proactivity in Prioritization Review Processes

In addition to managing challenges, heterogeneous teams must also be proactive in the review of priorities. This means they should not wait for problems to manifest before reviewing their priorities, but should be able to identify potential changes in project or market needs and act accordingly.

One way to promote this proactivity is to establish regular review moments, even when there is no immediate crisis to address. For instance, teams can schedule strategic review sprints, during which project progress is examined, and new opportunities or risks are considered. This proactive approach to prioritization review allows teams to remain aligned with overall objectives, reducing the risk of unexpected deviations.

8.4.4 Developing Adaptability in Team Members

To promote effective adaptation in heterogeneous teams, it is necessary to develop adaptability not only at the group level but also at the individual level. Each team member should feel empowered to manage changes and actively contribute to the adaptation process. This can be facilitated through continuous training initiatives and coaching, which help team members enhance their technical and relational skills.

Promoting continuous learning and providing tools for personal skill development not only improves team effectiveness but also increases the resilience of the group as a whole. Members who feel confident in their adaptability skills are more likely to collaborate actively during periods of change and provide valuable contributions to the success of the project.

8.4.5 Conclusion on Adaptation and Proactivity in Heterogeneous Teams

Continuous adaptation and proactivity are essential tools for the success of heterogeneous teams. Promoting a culture of continuous adaptation, anticipating challenges, and fostering proactivity in prioritization review allows teams to respond quickly to changes without losing direction. This approach not only enhances the team's ability to address unforeseen situations but also strengthens internal cohesion and mutual trust, ensuring that the team remains flexible and ready to tackle new challenges successfully.

8.5. Conclusion of the Chapter: Adaptation as a Tool for Success in Heterogeneous Teams

Continuous adaptation is a key competency for the success of a heterogeneous team. The cultural, technical, and operational differences within a group can pose significant challenges, but with the right approach, they can also become a source of strength and innovation. Addressing change and continuously revising priorities in a structured and proactive manner enables teams to navigate complexities and changes more effectively and cohesively.

8.5.1 Integrating Adaptation into Work Routines

One of the main lessons from this chapter is that adaptation should not be seen as an extraordinary reaction to unforeseen events but as an integral part of the work routine. In heterogeneous teams, where the variety of skills and experiences can lead to conflicting views on priorities, integrating adaptation into the project lifecycle is essential to ensure that the team remains aligned and focused on common objectives.

Through tools such as regular backlog reviews and priority assessments, inclusive facilitation, and the use of shared metrics, teams can maintain a clear view of their priorities and adapt flexibly to new needs. This not only improves operational efficiency but also fosters a more collaborative and harmonious work environment, where every team member feels involved and valued.

8.5.2 Creating a Continuous Feedback Loop

A fundamental element for the success of adaptation in heterogeneous teams is the establishment of a continuous feedback loop. Feedback should not be limited to retrospective phases but should become an ongoing process that allows team members to express their concerns, propose improvements, and reflect on achieved goals. This continuous flow of information ensures that decisions are based on concrete data and shared experiences, reducing the risk of misunderstandings or miscommunications.

In heterogeneous teams, where cultural and operational differences can complicate communication, continuous feedback helps maintain alignment and prevents issues from arising before they become difficult to manage. Additionally, it provides an opportunity to make real-time corrections, thereby enhancing the team's ability to respond promptly to challenges.

8.5.3 Enhancing Team Resilience

The ability to adapt involves not only managing change in the immediate sense but also building long-term resilience. In heterogeneous teams, where complexity is heightened due to diverse skills and cultural perspectives, developing resilience is crucial to ensure that the team can handle not only current changes but also future ones.

Resilience is built through practices such as continuous training, fostering an active learning environment, and adopting an iterative approach that allows the team to evolve constantly. Team members accustomed to managing change smoothly and consistently develop a greater capacity to face new challenges with confidence and proactivity.

8.5.4 Conclusion of the Chapter

In conclusion, the process of adaptation in heterogeneous teams is a fundamental component of their success. The adoption of proactive practices, the creation of continuous feedback loops, and the integration of adaptation into daily routines enable teams to navigate the complexities of change more effectively. Adaptation is not merely a response to immediate challenges but a working model that ensures greater resilience and cohesion in the long term. With this approach, heterogeneous teams can not only manage change successfully but also leverage it as a catalyst for enhancing their performance and capacity for innovation.

Chapter 9

The Value of Reflection and Continuous Improvement in Heterogeneous Teams

Chapter 9 - The Value of Reflection and Continuous Improvement in Heterogeneous Teams

Chapter 9 - The Value of Reflection and Continuous Improvement in Heterogeneous Teams

The concept of continuous reflection is one of the most critical aspects of any agile methodology, as it provides the team with the opportunity to analyze what went well and what can be improved. In heterogeneous teams, this process becomes even more important and, at the same time, more complex due to the differences in cultural, experiential, and technical backgrounds among the members. In this chapter, we will explore the challenges of reflection and continuous improvement in a heterogeneous context and how teams can effectively address them. We will also include a case study on a team operating across multiple countries with different regulatory requirements, demonstrating how retrospectives and iterative improvement were successfully managed in a multicultural setting.

9.1. The Value of Continuous Reflection in Heterogeneous Teams

In agile teams, continuous reflection, represented by retrospectives, is a fundamental practice for constantly improving processes, outcomes, and internal dynamics. However, in heterogeneous teams, this practice can encounter several challenges arising from the diversity of backgrounds, skills, and cultures. Reflection thus becomes a critical moment where divergences must be addressed constructively, always aiming for continuous improvement.

9.1.1. Challenges of Retrospectives in Heterogeneous Teams

The first challenge in conducting effective retrospectives in heterogeneous teams concerns cultural differences. In some cultures, direct critical feedback is considered normal and acceptable, while in others it may be perceived as rude or disrespectful. This means that during retrospectives, some members may feel uncomfortable openly sharing their opinions or criticizing the work of others, fearing they might offend or be viewed negatively.

Another common difficulty in distributed or multinational teams is linguistic barriers. When the team does not share the same native language, expressing detailed and complex feedback can become difficult, leading to misunderstandings or a lack of clarity on important issues. In such contexts, there is a risk that some ideas or concerns may not be expressed correctly or may be misinterpreted by other team members.

Moreover, there are differences in expectations regarding problem resolution. Some members may prefer quick and immediate solutions, while others may want to thoroughly analyze the root causes of issues before implementing changes. These divergences in expectations can create friction within the team and make it challenging to find common ground for decision-making.

9.1.2. Solutions to Improve Participation

To overcome these challenges, it is essential that retrospectives are managed inclusively and consider the cultural and linguistic differences present within the team. One of the most effective solutions is to adopt a facilitated approach. An experienced facilitator, whether internal or external to the team, can help moderate discussions so that everyone has the opportunity to contribute and do so without fear. The facilitator can use tools such as round robin, where each team member has their moment to speak, or anonymous voting techniques to highlight sensitive issues without exposing individuals directly.

Another effective method is to use asynchronous collaboration tools. Platforms like Trello, Miro, or Confluence allow team members to share their thoughts and feedback in advance, giving everyone time to reflect and articulate their responses clearly, overcoming language or time zone barriers. This practice also reduces pressure during live retrospectives, as the main ideas have already been expressed and can be discussed more easily.

Finally, to enhance participation in retrospectives, it is crucial to establish a culture of psychological safety within the team. Members must feel free to express their opinions without fear of judgment. To create this culture, team leaders must be the first to promote open and honest dialogue, demonstrating through their behavior that feedback, even critical, is always welcomed constructively, and that differing opinions are viewed as an added value rather than a hindrance.

In conclusion, in heterogeneous teams, continuous reflection can be challenging, but with the use of facilitation techniques, asynchronous collaboration tools, and the promotion of a culture of psychological safety, these difficulties can be overcome. Creating a space where all members feel free to actively participate not only improves the quality of retrospectives but also strengthens the sense of belonging and cohesion within the team, leading to continuous improvement that involves everyone.

9.2. Implementing Continuous Improvement in Heterogeneous Teams

Implementing continuous improvement is a central aspect of agile methodologies, and in heterogeneous teams, it requires special attention. After each retrospective, the feedback collected must be translated into concrete actions to improve processes and outcomes. However, due to cultural, operational, and work approach differences, this phase can be more complex in heterogeneous teams compared to homogeneous ones. In this section, we will explore the challenges that arise in implementing continuous improvement and how to overcome them.

9.2.1. Differences in Interpretation and Adoption of Change

One of the main challenges in heterogeneous teams is that different members may have divergent opinions on what constitutes a true "improvement." In some disciplines, a change may be seen as progress, while in others, it may be perceived as an additional complication. For example, software developers might view the automation of a process as an improvement, whereas less technical team members might see it as a challenge to be addressed.

Moreover, cultural differences can influence how team members react to changes. Some cultures tend to value stability and continuity, preferring minimal modifications, while others might be more oriented toward change and innovation. This contrast can lead to difficulties in adopting proposed changes during retrospectives, slowing down the improvement process.

To address these differences, it is essential to establish shared criteria for evaluating what constitutes an improvement. These criteria should be defined collaboratively so that all team members understand and accept the success metrics. For instance, indicators such as reduced delivery times, improved product quality, or decreased errors could be established as key elements for measuring improvement. Using clear and quantifiable KPIs (Key Performance Indicators) helps avoid subjective discussions and ensures that all team members are aligned on the same objectives.

9.2.2. Monitoring and Reviewing Changes

Once changes have been implemented, it is crucial to regularly monitor progress and assess the effectiveness of the modifications made. In heterogeneous teams, it is important that this monitoring process is transparent and accessible to all team members, regardless of their technical skills or role.

To make monitoring more effective, teams can use tools like dashboards or visual metrics that allow real-time visualization of the impact of changes. For example, a dashboard showing the decrease in bugs or the increase in delivery speed can help team members clearly see the results of the changes, fostering greater acceptance and understanding of the implemented improvements.

Follow-up sessions are another useful tool for evaluating changes. These meetings allow the team to discuss progress made, analyze any difficulties encountered, and decide if further adjustments are necessary. In heterogeneous teams, these sessions must be facilitated to ensure that every member can express their opinions, making sure that different perspectives are taken into consideration.

9.2.3. Active Involvement of All Team Members

To ensure that continuous improvement is effective in heterogeneous teams, it is essential that all team members are involved in the process. Often, members with fewer technical skills or those belonging to disciplines not directly related to development may feel excluded from change decisions. This can lead to a lack of adoption of changes or a decrease in motivation.

To avoid this, it is important to actively engage all team members, making sure that the improvement process is seen as a collective action rather than a decision made solely by one part of the team. Using facilitation techniques, such as group meetings where every member has the opportunity to share their ideas and proposals, can foster greater involvement.

In conclusion, implementing continuous improvement in heterogeneous teams requires a structured and inclusive approach. Establishing clear criteria for evaluating improvements, monitoring progress transparently, and actively involving all team members are fundamental practices to ensure the success of the improvement process. Addressing cultural and operational differences with an open and collaborative mindset allows teams to transform these diversities into an advantage, continuously improving processes and achieving superior results.

9.3. Case Study: A Team Operating Across Multiple Countries with Different Regulatory

To better understand how heterogeneous teams can address the challenges of continuous reflection and iterative improvement, it is useful to analyze a real case study. In this example, a multinational team operating in different countries, each with its own regulations and standards, faced numerous difficulties in managing a global software development project. The team, composed of members from various nationalities and disciplines, successfully overcame the complexities arising from regulatory and cultural differences by adopting a structured approach to continuous improvement and reflection.

9.3.1. Initial Challenges: Regulatory and Cultural Differences

The primary challenges this team faced stemmed from regulatory differences and cultural barriers. Each nation involved in the project had specific regulatory requirements regarding software development and compliance. For instance, while one country required strict adherence to data protection regulations, others had less stringent rules, creating a divergence of priorities and expectations.

Additionally, the cultural differences among team members further complicated the reflection and continuous improvement process. Some members came from cultures where direct and critical feedback was encouraged, while others preferred to avoid open confrontation, opting for a more diplomatic and discreet approach. These differences initially made the reflection process during retrospectives challenging, leading to a slowdown in the adoption of necessary changes.

9.3.2. Solution: Facilitation and Alignment through Reference Standards

To overcome these difficulties, the team adopted a series of practical solutions that effectively managed both regulatory and cultural differences. The first measure taken was the appointment of an experienced facilitator tasked with moderating retrospectives and continuous improvement meetings. The facilitator's role was to create an environment where all team members felt comfortable expressing their opinions, regardless of cultural differences. By using techniques like anonymous feedback collection and silent voting, the team was able to overcome the cultural barriers that hindered open discussion.

Another crucial measure was the introduction of shared reference standards to ensure regulatory alignment across different jurisdictions. Instead of trying to meet the regulations of each country separately, the team decided to develop a common regulatory framework that satisfied the most stringent requirements among those involved. This approach allowed the team to avoid duplication of efforts and reduce discrepancies, creating a common foundation to work from.

9.3.3. Benefits of the Iterative Improvement Process

The adoption of a structured and facilitated approach to reflection and continuous improvement brought numerous benefits to the team. Firstly, the retrospective process became much more inclusive. Thanks to the anonymization of feedback and expert facilitation, team members who previously felt uncomfortable expressing criticism began to participate more actively in discussions, bringing a wide range of perspectives and suggestions.

Furthermore, creating a common regulatory standard significantly simplified the management of complexities related to various regulations. This allowed the team to work more efficiently, reducing review and approval times while ensuring that all parts of the project complied with local laws. The team was able to avoid significant delays due to regulatory checks, allowing for increased development speed.

Continuous monitoring of improvements also enabled the team to see the positive impact of the changes made. By using dashboards and regular reports, team members could observe in real-time the evolution of performance and product quality improvements. This led to increased motivation and reinforced the sense of belonging to the project.

9.3.4. Lessons Learned and Future Impacts

One of the most important lessons learned from this case study is that, in heterogeneous teams, continuous reflection and iterative improvement must be structured to work effectively. Facilitation, the creation of common standards, and the adoption of techniques that respect cultural and regulatory differences are essential elements to ensure that all team members can contribute and that changes are implemented efficiently.

This approach allowed the team to successfully navigate the complexity of working in an international environment and established a solid foundation for future projects. Through this process, the team developed greater resilience and adaptability, which proved crucial for tackling future challenges, both regulatory and operational.

9.3.5. Conclusion of the Case Study

The case study of the multinational team operating in multiple countries with different regulatory requirements demonstrates how continuous reflection and iterative improvement can be effectively implemented even in heterogeneous teams facing significant complexities. Through structured facilitation, the creation of shared standards, and ongoing monitoring, the team managed to overcome cultural and regulatory differences, enhancing its performance and ensuring project success.

Chapter 9 - The Value of Reflection and Continuous Improvement in Heterogeneous Teams

9.4. Adaptation and Proactivity in Heterogeneous Teams

Continuous adaptation is an essential practice for ensuring that heterogeneous teams remain flexible and responsive to change. However, in teams composed of members with diverse cultural, technical, and operational backgrounds, it is important to go beyond mere reactive adaptation. These teams must be proactive, anticipating challenges and strategically planning responses while leveraging diversity as a resource to navigate complexities.

9.4.1. Creating a Culture of Continuous Adaptation

A culture of continuous adaptation is key to keeping heterogeneous teams resilient and ready to meet challenges. In teams where cultural and operational differences can lead to varying interpretations of changes and priorities, promoting a mindset of constant adaptation is crucial. The goal is not simply to react to changes but to anticipate them and transform them into growth opportunities.

To foster this culture, leaders must encourage an open mindset and willingness to modify plans and strategies as necessary. Retrospectives and reflection moments should be regularly integrated into the team's routines, aiming to identify not only what went wrong but also what could be proactively improved.

Adopting a culture that embraces change as an integral part of daily work reduces internal resistance and enhances the team's ability to face new challenges without anxiety or difficulty. In heterogeneous teams, where diverse opinions can enrich the reflection process, this approach is particularly useful for fostering innovation and collaboration.

9.4.2. Anticipating Challenges and Preparing for Change

In heterogeneous teams, challenges can be particularly complex due to the diverse perspectives, skills, and cultural contexts of the members. However, one of the main advantages of a heterogeneous team is its ability to anticipate difficulties and tackle them proactively, thanks to the variety of viewpoints present.

To this end, it is beneficial to organize risk forecasting sessions that involve all team members, during which potential future challenges are examined, and contingency plans are developed. During these sessions, team members can highlight issues that others might not have considered, thereby enriching the group's ability to prepare for change.

This proactive approach helps the team avoid being caught off guard by unforeseen problems and maintains a proactive attitude even in complex situations. In heterogeneous teams, where communication and understanding of priorities may be more difficult, the ability to anticipate challenges becomes even more valuable.

9.4.3. Facilitating Proactivity in the Prioritization Review Process

Being proactive also means effectively managing the review of priorities in advance. In heterogeneous teams, where viewpoints on priorities can be very different, it is essential that reviews do not only occur in response to problems or sudden changes but are scheduled regularly and conducted in a structured manner.

A useful strategy is to establish fixed times for reviewing priorities, during which the team proactively examines the goals and needs of the project, without waiting for a crisis to emerge. This approach allows for structured flexibility, in which change is managed proactively rather than as a reaction to sudden events.

In prioritization review sessions, the team should also consider contextual or market changes that might impact the project. Adopting competitive analysis tools and performance metrics allows for the early evaluation of whether priorities need to be adjusted to adapt to new conditions or opportunities.

9.4.4. Developing Adaptation Skills Among Team Members

For a heterogeneous team to manage change effectively, each team member must develop their own adaptation skills. This means being able not only to react to changes but also to feel comfortable proposing modifications, experimenting with new ideas, and learning from mistakes.

Continuous training plays a fundamental role in this process. Organizing targeted learning sessions and workshops on soft skills and change management helps team members feel more confident in dealing with uncertainty. Specifically, adopting an iterative approach to learning, where lessons are drawn from mistakes and gradual improvements are implemented, allows team members to grow and continuously enhance their skills.

Promoting a culture of learning and providing continuous support to team members creates an environment where change is seen not as a threat but as an opportunity for growth and innovation. In heterogeneous teams, this adaptability becomes a competitive advantage, enabling the group to successfully navigate the complexities of the project and the external context.

9.4.5. Conclusion on Adaptation and Proactivity in Heterogeneous Teams

Continuous adaptation and proactivity are essential elements for the success of heterogeneous teams. Creating a culture that promotes adaptation as an integral part of daily work and encourages team members to be proactive in reviewing priorities and addressing challenges is fundamental to ensuring that the team remains flexible and resilient. The adoption of risk forecasting sessions, continuous training, and a structured review process enables the team to not only respond to changes effectively but also to leverage them as opportunities for growth and improvement.

Chapter 10

Maintaining Strategic Vision in Heterogeneous Teams

Chapter 10 - Maintaining Strategic Vision in Heterogeneous Teams

10.1 The Strategic Vision in an Agile Environment

In an agile environment, the main challenge is to reconcile the need for flexibility and responsiveness with maintaining a clear and long-term strategic vision. Unlike more traditional methodologies, such as the Waterfall model, where strategic planning occurs upfront and remains unchanged until the end of the project, the agile approach encourages continuous adaptation. This requires teams to work in iterative cycles, with constant revisions of priorities. However, this ongoing evolution should not obscure the long-term objectives.

10.1.1 The Paradox of Agility: Flexibility vs. Strategic Vision

Agility is often seen as synonymous with immediate adaptability to changes, whether internal or external. However, a common mistake is to think that agility equates to a lack of strategic direction. On the contrary, the true strength of agility lies in finding a balance between maintaining a coherent strategic vision and being adaptable in the short term. This is particularly important for heterogeneous teams, where diverse skills and perspectives can lead to fragmentation if not adequately aligned with a shared objective.

In this context, excessive flexibility risks compromising strategic coherence, while too much rigidity could prevent teams from responding swiftly to evolving market needs.

Heterogeneous teams must confront this challenge acutely, as each team member may perceive the strategic vision differently based on their role, background, or expertise.

10.1.2 Defining a Sustainable Strategic Vision

To maintain a sustainable strategic vision in an agile environment, the first step is to define a clear long-term direction that guides all activities without being overly specific or rigid. The strategic vision should answer fundamental questions such as:

- What business value do we want to generate?
- Where do we want to be in 1, 3, or 5 years?
- How can we measure success concerning this vision?

These answers provide a framework within which teams can operate agilely, adapting daily activities in response to changes while keeping an eye on the ultimate goal.

The strategic vision must also be communicated clearly at all levels of the team. In a heterogeneous team, members may have different interpretations of the same vision, making it crucial for this vision to be reiterated constantly during meetings and coordination sessions. Aligning around the vision is a continuous process that needs to be reinforced through the use of roadmaps, milestones, and shared objectives.

10.1.3 Strategic Iteration and Agility

A winning strategy cannot be static; it must evolve with the context in which it operates. However, the process of strategic iteration must be managed carefully. Too many changes to the strategy can create confusion or diminish the team's trust in the business direction. Conversely, a strategic vision that does not evolve risks becoming obsolete in a rapidly changing market.

Strategic iteration should not be confused with constant adjustments to every aspect of the vision. The key is to make incremental adjustments based on real and measurable feedback while keeping the primary direction intact. This way, teams can continue to work from a solid foundation without feeling constantly disoriented by strategic changes.

A concrete example might be updating a strategic roadmap quarterly based on achieved results and relevant market or technological changes. This roadmap provides a clear reference point that allows teams to see how their daily activities fit into the broader strategic context.

10.1.4 Short-term and Long-term Goals

In Agile Synergy, a good practice is the division between short-term goals (for sprint cycles or quarters) and long-term goals (for the entire project or organization). This division allows teams to work efficiently in the short term while maintaining focus on the final objectives.

Short-term goals may involve improving specific features, reducing bugs, or implementing new functionalities requested by customers. In contrast, long-term objectives might include expanding into new markets, developing a more scalable platform, or continuously optimizing user experience.

To ensure that these two sets of objectives do not conflict, it is essential to have periodic verification mechanisms, such as strategic retrospectives or alignment meetings between leadership and operational teams. These moments allow recalibrating the strategic focus and ensuring that everyone is working toward the same purpose.

10.1.5 The Role of Leadership in Strategic Vision

The leadership team plays a crucial role in balancing vision and agility. Their task is not only to establish the strategic direction but also to act as a constant link between the long-term vision and the daily activities of the teams. They must communicate clearly and inspire teams to understand that every iteration and decision contributes to the bigger picture.

This type of leadership requires an integrated view of business and technology, where communication is key to maintaining alignment between strategy and operations. In a heterogeneous context, continuous cultural adaptation is also necessary so that teams feel a sense of active participation in achieving the strategic vision.

10.2. Balancing Strategic Vision with Operational Agility

Balancing strategic vision and operational agility is an essential challenge for heterogeneous teams. While the strategic vision provides clear long-term direction, operational agility allows teams to respond swiftly to changes or unexpected events. Success lies in the ability to combine these two seemingly opposing elements.

10.2.1 Operational Agility in Heterogeneous Teams

In heterogeneous teams, diverse skill sets can lead to variable approaches to daily operations. Members with technical backgrounds may prioritize immediate efficiency, while those with business expertise may focus on strategic objectives. The challenge is to harmonize these approaches to ensure that operational flexibility does not compromise the strategic vision.

An example can be found in software development teams that, if focused exclusively on resolving bugs or delivering newly requested functionalities in the short term, may deviate from the strategic roadmap. This highlights the importance of managing the backlog strategically, ensuring that operational tasks align with long-term objectives.

10.2.2 Tools to Align Strategy and Operations

To maintain this balance, it is essential to adopt tools and practices that promote transparency and continuous alignment. Among these:

1. Visual Roadmaps: Roadmaps help keep the entire team aligned with long-term objectives. They should be regularly updated and visible to everyone, allowing the team to understand how daily activities connect to the overall strategy.
2. OKRs (Objectives and Key Results): Using OKRs can help break down the strategic vision into measurable short-term objectives, making operational work more focused and driven by concrete results.
3. Strategic Retrospectives: In addition to regular retrospectives that focus on team efficiency, it is beneficial to introduce strategy-oriented retrospectives. These moments allow for reflection not only on short-term results but also on alignment with strategic objectives.

10.2.3 Leadership and Operational Agility

The role of leadership is to facilitate change while keeping the team on course toward strategic objectives. Leaders must interpret changing priorities without losing sight of long-term impact. They serve as guides and filters, deciding which tactical changes can be accepted without deviating from the broader vision.

To achieve this, leadership must encourage constant communication between operational and managerial teams, ensuring that every level of the team is well aware of how daily activities contribute to high-level goals.

This section provides guidance on how to balance the need for rapid and flexible responses to new challenges while maintaining focus on broader strategic objectives. The use of roadmaps, OKRs, and strategic retrospectives helps ensure that agility and strategy do not exclude each other.

10.3. Managing Divergences Between Vision and Operations

Another key challenge for heterogeneous teams is managing the divergences between the strategic vision and daily operational needs. These divergences can manifest when immediate activities clash with long-term objectives, requiring careful management to avoid conflicts that hinder progress.

10.3.1 Identifying and Understanding Divergences

The first step in managing divergences is to identify them early. Divergences can arise from various causes, including:

- Conflicting Priorities: Operational teams may feel pressured to respond to urgent requests that, while important in the short term, can divert attention from the strategic roadmap.

- Different Perspectives: Team members, coming from diverse backgrounds, may have differing opinions on how to address certain problems. Those focused on technology might prioritize innovation, while the business team might concentrate on immediate economic returns.

10.3.2 Tools to Mitigate Divergences

To effectively manage the divergences between operations and strategy, it is essential to adopt tools and processes that facilitate dialogue and mediation among different interests:

1. Strategic Workshops: Organizing periodic workshops where team members can openly discuss divergences and find common solutions. This allows for understanding how to adapt operations to strategic goals, reducing the risk of deviations.
2. Continuous Feedback Loops: Creating constant feedback flows, both operationally and strategically, helps maintain balance. Frequent feedback between development teams, leadership, and stakeholders allows for recalibrating operational priorities in light of strategic objectives.
3. Realignment Meetings: Scheduling regular meetings dedicated to realigning operations and strategy helps correct any deviations. During these sessions, the team can evaluate whether short-term activities are effectively contributing to strategic goals.

10.3.3 The Role of Leaders in Divergences

Leaders play a critical role in mediating and managing divergences between vision and operations. They must be able to:

• Provide Clarity: When conflicts arise between operational needs and strategic objectives, it is the leadership's responsibility to provide clear direction to keep the team focused on the most important goals.

• Encourage Compromise: Leaders should promote compromise, seeking solutions that effectively balance operational urgency with the long-term vision.

Managing divergences between operations and strategy requires a combination of continuous dialogue, flexibility, and proactive leadership. The use of tools such as workshops, feedback, and realignment meetings helps reduce conflicts and maintain focus on long-term objectives.

10.4. Maintaining Consistency in Vision Across Diverse Teams

In a heterogeneous team context, maintaining consistency in the strategic vision can be complex, especially when teams operate in different areas or have varying priorities and competencies. Ensuring that all team members are aligned toward a common goal is crucial for long-term success.

10.4.1 Transparent and Ongoing Communication

One of the keys to maintaining consistency in vision is transparent and ongoing communication. Here are some effective approaches:

• Periodic Alignment Meetings: Organizing regular meetings to reiterate the strategic vision and ensure that each team understands how their daily activities contribute to achieving it. These sessions help renew collective commitment toward common objectives.

• Sharing Strategic Documents: Providing access to documents that clearly explain the vision, goals, and corporate values can reinforce understanding of the long-term strategy. These documents serve as a constant reference for every team member.

10.4.2 Creating Links Between Short- and Long-Term Goals

Maintaining consistency requires that teams understand how short-term objectives connect to the overall strategic vision:

1. Shared Roadmap: Creating a roadmap that clearly shows the connections between short-term milestones and long-term strategic goals. This visualization helps teams see how their daily activities fit into the broader picture.
2. Defined Intermediate Goals: Establishing intermediate goals that bridge immediate outcomes and the final vision. These objectives help teams stay focused on the long term while maintaining a sense of tangible progress.

10.4.3 The Role of Leadership in Consistency

Leadership plays a fundamental role in maintaining consistency in vision across different teams. Leaders must:

•   Ensure Message Cohesion: Leaders need to consistently communicate the strategic vision with a coherent message, avoiding ambiguous interpretations that could lead teams astray.

•   Promote an Inclusive Vision: They must be able to adapt the strategic vision to different contexts, making it relevant for each team. This increases motivation and alignment among teams with different functions or priorities.

10.4.4 Continuous Monitoring and Feedback

Finally, maintaining consistency requires regular monitoring and continuous feedback:

•   Measure Progress Against the Vision: Teams should regularly monitor their progress relative to the strategic roadmap to ensure their activities align with the overall vision.

•   Adjust the Course When Necessary: Consistency does not mean rigidity. If changes occur in the external environment or corporate priorities, the strategic vision must be adapted while still keeping the final objective in sight.

Maintaining consistency in the strategic vision across diverse teams requires transparent communication, clear intermediate objectives, and strong leadership. Through constant monitoring and continuous feedback, teams can align their operations with long-term goals, contributing to overall success.

10.5. Promoting Autonomy While Maintaining Alignment with Vision

Team autonomy is a fundamental value in an agile environment, but it is essential to ensure that this autonomy does not compromise alignment with the strategic vision. Balancing operational independence with consistency regarding corporate direction requires a structured and collaborative approach.

10.5.1. Autonomy with Clear Boundaries

To promote productive autonomy, it is necessary to establish clear boundaries within which teams can operate:

- Well-Defined Objectives: Leaders must provide clear and measurable goals while allowing teams the freedom to determine how to achieve them. This enables teams to explore innovative solutions while still focusing on strategic objectives.
- Decentralized Decision-Making: Encourage a decentralized decision-making model where teams can

make daily decisions without requiring constant approvals, as long as they remain aligned with overarching goals.

10.5.2. Strategic Alignment Tools

To maintain alignment between autonomous teams and the overall strategic vision, it is essential to have appropriate tools:

- **Alignment Frameworks:** Utilize tools like OKRs (Objectives and Key Results) or similar methodologies that help keep the strategic vision visible and tangible for everyone. OKRs, for example, allow for clear objective setting for each team, while monitoring key results ensures that teams stay on track.
- **Shared Dashboards:** Implement visible dashboards for all teams that display real-time progress toward business goals. These tools make performance clear and tangible, holding teams accountable for their contributions.

10.5.3. Feedback and Transparency Culture

Promoting a culture of open feedback is essential for balancing autonomy and alignment:

- **Continuous Feedback:** Autonomous teams must be consistently informed of their impact and receive regular feedback. Timely feedback allows for corrections if deviations from the strategic vision occur and reinforces what is working well.
- **Transparency in Results:** Ensure that all teams are aware of common objectives and how each group is contributing. Transparency in performance fosters a sense of accountability and motivation to stay aligned.

10.5.4. Leadership as Strategic Guidance

Finally, leaders must act as facilitators to ensure that the operational autonomy of teams does not compromise alignment with the vision:

- Monitoring and Support: Leaders need to observe how autonomous teams are progressing toward business objectives and intervene only when necessary, providing strategic support without micromanaging.
- Sense of Collective Responsibility: Encourage team leaders to see themselves as custodians of the strategic vision, guiding their groups to make decisions that support the organization's overall mission.

Promoting team autonomy requires a carefully managed balance. With clear objectives, effective alignment tools, and a culture of transparency and feedback, teams can enjoy operational freedom without losing sight of the common strategic direction.

10.6. Continuous Adaptation to the Strategic Vision

Agility requires constant adaptation to the strategic vision to respond to market changes, new opportunities, and emerging challenges. It is crucial for teams to have the ability to quickly update their actions and seamlessly align with the corporate direction.

10.6.1 Monitoring the Vision and Context

Effective management of continuous adaptation requires constant monitoring of the context and strategy:

• Regular Vision Assessment: The strategic vision should not be viewed as a fixed point but rather as a dynamic objective. Teams must periodically review the strategic direction and verify its consistency with current realities.

• External Context Scanning: Teams need mechanisms to monitor market conditions, technological evolution, and customer needs to proactively update their activities and adapt accordingly.

10.6.2 Agile Adaptation of Priorities

To stay aligned with the vision, teams must frequently adjust their priorities in response to internal and external changes:

• Frequent Review Cycles: Include strategic adjustments in sprints or quarterly planning to ensure that short-term priorities reflect the updated strategic direction.

• Rapid Redirecting: Encourage an approach that allows for the quick reallocation of resources and objectives if the strategy or vision changes. This enables the exploitation of emerging opportunities and mitigation of unforeseen risks.

10.6.3 Feedback as a Driver of Adaptation

Continuous feedback fuels the capacity for adaptation, allowing teams to correct their course and evolve with the vision:

• Result Evaluation: Regularly analyze the results achieved against strategic objectives to identify discrepancies and opportunities for improvement. Feedback on ongoing projects should inform strategic decisions.

• Iteration Based on Feedback: Use internal and external feedback to quickly adjust activities, ensuring that every change in the strategic vision is reflected in daily operations.

10.6.4 Flexible and Visionary Leadership

Leaders must play a crucial role in guiding teams through adaptation:

• Updated Vision: Leaders must be ready to review and clearly communicate the updated vision, ensuring that all teams understand the new direction and its operational implications.

- Adaptive Coaching: Instead of imposing changes from the top, leaders should act as coaches, helping teams internalize modifications and adapt their priorities and processes.

Continuous adaptation is essential to ensure that teams remain flexible and ready to respond to the evolution of corporate strategy. With constant monitoring, regular feedback, and visionary leadership, teams can agilely navigate challenges while maintaining alignment with the overall strategic direction.

Chapter 10 - Maintaining Strategic Vision in Heterogeneous Teams

Chapter 11
Collaboration and Innovation in Diverse Teams

Chapter 11 - Collaboration and Innovation in Diverse Teams

In a complex business context, collaboration and innovation play a central role, especially when teams are composed of members with different skills and backgrounds. This chapter analyzes how to facilitate collaboration and promote innovation in diverse teams, exploring common difficulties and existing solutions to maximize operational effectiveness.

11.1. Challenges in Collaboration Among Diverse Teams

Diverse teams, composed of members with different skills, cultural backgrounds, and viewpoints, are a valuable resource, but they can also encounter various challenges in collaboration. Successfully overcoming these challenges is crucial for creating a productive environment capable of maximizing the benefits of diversity and fostering innovation.

11.1.1. Communication Barriers

One of the main difficulties in diverse teams relates to communication. Language barriers, cultural differences, and varying communication styles can create misunderstandings and slow down the work process. These obstacles can negatively impact group cohesion and the ability to collaborate effectively.

Solutions:

• Structured communication channels: Establish clear and formal communication channels to promote a continuous and well-organized flow of information. Digital tools like Slack or Microsoft Teams can be used to centralize communications and ensure that everyone is updated on progress.

• Cross-cultural training: Invest in training to improve understanding of cultural differences and raise awareness among team members about more inclusive communication styles.

• Use of simple language: Encourage the use of clear and straightforward language, avoiding technical jargon or ambiguous expressions that could create confusion.

11.1.2. Alignment of Objectives

In a diverse team, each member may have different priorities, expectations, and goals based on their role, professional background, and past experiences. This misalignment can create tension, confusion, and slowdowns in project progress.

Solutions:

• Define clear and shared objectives: At the beginning of each project, it is essential to align all members around a common vision. This translates into clearly defined objectives that are understood and accepted by everyone.

• Regular alignment sessions: Periodic meetings, such as sprint reviews or workshops, can be useful to ensure that team members remain focused on project objectives and make necessary adjustments in response to changes.

11.1.3. Managing Differences in Skills

The diversity of technical skills and professional backgrounds is a strength of mixed teams, but it can also represent a challenge when team members struggle to understand each other's competencies or to integrate them effectively into group work.

Solutions:

• Facilitate mutual understanding: Organize workshops or cross-functional training sessions to promote a better understanding of each team member's skills. These sessions help members see how different competencies can contribute to the project's success.

• Define clear roles and responsibilities: It is important that each team member clearly understands their role and how their skills integrate with those of others. This helps avoid task overlaps and improves overall work effectiveness.

11.1.4. Conflict Resolution

Differences in viewpoints, work approaches, and expectations can generate internal conflicts. If not managed correctly, these conflicts can erode trust and compromise the productivity of the team.

Solutions:

• Create an open and trusting environment: Promote a team culture in which conflicts are seen as opportunities to improve collaboration. This includes encouraging open and honest discussions, where differences can be expressed and addressed constructively.

- Leadership in conflict mediation: Team leaders must be prepared to intervene quickly when conflicts arise, facilitating resolution through mediation techniques and active dialogue. A leader who promotes mutual respect and cooperation helps the team overcome difficulties.

11.2. Strategies to Promote Collaboration in Diverse Teams

Collaboration in diverse teams requires the adoption of specific strategies that facilitate the integration of skills and perspectives, fostering a cohesive and productive environment. When well implemented, these strategies help build a climate of trust and mutual respect, fundamental elements for the success of a varied team.

11.2.1. Create Collaborative Spaces

A fundamental aspect of promoting collaboration in diverse teams is ensuring the availability of spaces, whether physical or digital, that allow team members to interact regularly and in a structured manner. Well-organized workspaces encourage the exchange of ideas and improve information sharing.

Solutions:

• Collaborative digital platforms: Tools like Confluence, Trello, and Slack are excellent for promoting collaboration in distributed teams. These platforms allow for the centralization of documents, discussions, and updates, making them accessible to all team members.

• Co-creation areas: Even in a physical environment, creating common spaces dedicated to co-creation, such as brainstorming rooms or flexible work areas, can encourage interaction and innovation.

11.2.2. Promote Team Building

Team building is essential for creating trust relationships and bringing out the individual qualities of each member. This can be achieved through structured activities aimed at improving communication and collaboration among team members.

Solutions:

• Workshops and team-building exercises: Specific activities designed to enhance mutual understanding and develop trust within the team. These moments help strengthen relationships and facilitate communication in everyday work situations.

• Informal moments: Organizing informal events, such as coffee breaks or team lunches, creates a more relaxed environment where members can get to know each other better outside the work context, improving cohesion.

11.2.3. Define Clear Roles and Responsibilities

In teams with varied competencies, it is important that each member knows exactly what their tasks and contributions to the project are. Well-defined roles and responsibilities help avoid overlaps, conflicts, and confusion, promoting smoother and more focused collaboration.

Solutions:

• Initial alignment meetings: At the beginning of a project, it is useful to take time to openly discuss the roles and responsibilities of each member, ensuring that everyone clearly understands their contribution and how it fits into the team's work.

• Regular progress updates: Weekly or bi-weekly meetings to review each member's progress and check whether roles need to be redefined or adapted to the emerging needs of the project.

11.2.4. Implement Reciprocal Mentoring

In diverse teams, reciprocal mentoring between members with different skills can foster personal and professional growth while simultaneously improving the group's collaborative capacity. Mentoring allows members to learn from each other, increasing understanding of each other's areas of expertise.

Solutions:

• Internal mentoring programs: Create a formal mentoring system within the team, where more experienced members on specific aspects can guide and support their colleagues. This not only helps fill skills gaps but also strengthens collaborative bonds.

• Peer-to-peer learning: Encouraging an environment where everyone is motivated to teach and learn from their colleagues, regardless of seniority level, promotes knowledge sharing and active collaboration.

11.2.5. Encourage Innovation through Diversity

Innovation in diverse teams can be actively stimulated by creating conditions for the free exchange of ideas and promoting a culture in which diversity is seen as an added value.

Solutions:

• Multidisciplinary brainstorming sessions: Organize regular meetings where members from different areas of expertise can share ideas and innovative solutions for ongoing projects. The diversity of viewpoints often generates creative and out-of-the-box solutions.

• Reward innovation: Establish a recognition system for innovative ideas, valuing each team member's contribution and fostering a climate of continuous improvement.

11.3. Managing Collaboration Challenges in Diverse Teams

Collaborating in diverse teams presents numerous challenges related to differences in skills, culture, and work styles. However, addressing these difficulties with targeted solutions allows for the transformation of such challenges into opportunities for growth and innovation. In this section, we analyze the main challenges and provide practical suggestions for overcoming them.

11.3.1. Overcoming Cultural Differences

Cultural differences can influence how team members communicate, make decisions, and handle conflict. Recognizing and managing these differences is crucial for effective collaboration.

Solutions:

• Cross-cultural training: Offer training sessions to help team members understand the different cultures represented in the group. This helps prevent misunderstandings and fosters an environment of mutual respect.

• Common codes of conduct: Establish shared rules for communication and conflict resolution, adapting these norms to the cultural sensitivities of team members. This creates common ground that facilitates interaction.

11.3.2. Managing Different Work Styles

In diverse teams, members often have different work styles: some may be more detail-oriented, while others may prefer a broader perspective. These differences can cause frustration if not managed correctly.

Solutions:

• Work style assessments: Use tools like the DISC test or Myers-Briggs to identify team members' work profiles. These tools help to better understand how each person prefers to work and interact with others.

• Task assignment based on styles: Assign tasks according to work styles, balancing activities between those who focus on details and those who prefer a broader view. This increases efficiency and reduces internal conflicts.

11.3.3. Resolving Conflicts Between Skills

When people with different professional backgrounds work together, misunderstandings regarding priorities and operational approaches may arise. It's important to find a balance between these complementary skills.

Solutions:

• Process facilitators: Introduce a facilitator or mediator to manage meetings or technical discussions. This person can help maintain focus on common goals, reducing conflicts between different skill sets.

• Project goal alignment: Periodically review project goals to ensure that all skills are aligned and that everyone understands how their work contributes to the bigger picture.

11.3.4. Managing Different Expectations

Team members may have differing expectations regarding deadlines, work quality, and responsibilities. These discrepancies can create tension within the group.

Solutions:

• Expectation clarification sessions: At the beginning of the project, it is helpful to openly discuss each member's expectations regarding the work. This helps to avoid future frustrations and establishes shared standards.

• Creation of detailed project plans: Define project plans that include deadlines, quality criteria, and individual responsibilities. This provides a clear framework for everyone, reducing the risk of misunderstandings.

11.3.5. Coordinating Remote Collaboration

Collaboration between distributed or remote teams can be an additional challenge in terms of communication and cohesion. The absence of face-to-face interaction makes it necessary to implement specific tools and techniques to keep the group connected.

Solutions:

• Advanced communication tools: Implement video conferencing, instant messaging, and document sharing tools to facilitate real-time communication among team members located in different locations.

• Regular virtual meetings: Schedule regular meetings to keep the team aligned on objectives and create a sense of belonging, even from a distance.

11.4. Fostering Creativity and Innovation in Diverse Teams

Diverse teams have great potential to stimulate creativity and innovation, thanks to the variety of skills and perspectives that members can offer. However, to realize this potential, it is necessary to create a favorable environment and adopt targeted strategies to cultivate innovative ideas. In this section, we explore how to facilitate creative processes and promote innovation in diverse teams.

11.4.1. Creating a Safe Space for Sharing Ideas

Creativity thrives best in an environment where team members feel comfortable sharing ideas without fear of being judged or criticized. In diverse contexts, cultural or skills barriers can inhibit the expression of ideas if not managed properly.

Strategies:

• Encouraging a culture of openness: Actively promote a culture where every team member is encouraged to propose ideas, even if they are not fully developed. Valuing diverse thinking and being open to unusual perspectives should be the foundation of daily collaboration.

• Structured brainstorming sessions: Organize brainstorming sessions where everyone has the space and time to freely express their ideas. Techniques such as "brainwriting" or "silent brainstorming" can encourage participation from all, especially those who tend to be less vocal.

11.4.2. Leveraging Diversity to Find Innovative Solutions

The variety of backgrounds and skills within a diverse team can provide a wide range of approaches to problems. This fosters the generation of innovative solutions that might not otherwise emerge in more homogeneous groups.

Strategies:

- Cross-pollination of skills: Encourage interaction among people with different skills to create a "pollination effect" across knowledge areas. Working together on common problems can lead to innovative solutions from unexpected perspectives.
- Multidisciplinary workshops: Organize workshops where teams from different disciplines collaborate on a common challenge. These workshops promote the discovery of synergies among various areas of expertise and stimulate new ideas.

11.4.3. Implementing Iterative Innovation Processes

Innovation does not stem solely from brilliant single ideas but often emerges from an iterative process of experimentation and improvement. In diverse teams, this approach is essential for refining and perfecting initial ideas through everyone's contributions.

Strategies:

- Rapid prototyping: Encourage the development of prototypes and preliminary versions of ideas for quick testing. Prototyping allows ideas to be put into practice and receive immediate feedback, stimulating continuous improvement.

• Regular feedback cycles: Integrate short, constant feedback cycles within the creative process, involving all team members. This allows for rapid adaptation of ideas and solutions based on insights gathered from people with different skills and viewpoints.

11.4.4. Promoting Distributed Leadership

Leadership in diverse teams should not be centralized. Distributing leadership among various team members, depending on their skills and the specific context, allows for better utilization of the group's creative potential.

Strategies:

• Rotation of leadership roles: Allow different team members to take on leadership roles based on their areas of expertise. This encourages empowerment and gives everyone the opportunity to lead innovative processes.

• Supporting innovation "champions": Identify and support individuals who naturally lean towards innovation, providing them with the tools and resources needed to advance their ideas and disseminate them within the team.

11.4.5. Balancing Creativity and Structure

While it is essential to promote creativity, it must be balanced with a clear structure to ensure that innovative ideas are realized and successfully implemented.

Strategies:

- Innovation framework: Implement a structured framework that guides creative processes without stifling innovation. Establish clear phases for generating, selecting, prototyping, and implementing ideas.
- Allocating time for innovation: Regularly schedule time dedicated to experimentation and innovation within the normal work cycle. This allows teams to explore new ideas without excessive pressure, maintaining a balance between innovation and daily activities.

By applying these strategies, diverse teams can develop a fertile environment for innovation and creativity, fully leveraging their different skills and perspectives to create innovative and impactful solutions.

11.5. Managing Conflicts in Diverse Teams

Diverse teams, while offering great potential for innovation, may encounter conflicts due to differences in opinions, cultures, work approaches, or communication styles. If not managed properly, these conflicts can hinder collaboration and compromise team effectiveness. However, when addressed constructively, conflicts can become an opportunity to improve mutual understanding and stimulate creative solutions. In this section, we explore how to manage conflicts within diverse teams.

11.5.1. Understanding the Causes of Conflicts

Effective conflict management begins with understanding its causes. In diverse teams, sources of conflict can be manifold, ranging from cultural differences to misunderstandings related to different work styles.

Main Causes of Conflict:

• Cultural differences: Each culture has its norms regarding communication, work approaches, time management, and problem-solving. These differences can lead to misunderstandings or clashes if they are not recognized and managed sensitively.

• Variety of skills and roles: In a heterogeneous team, each member may have a different perspective on how to address a problem, based on their technical and professional skills. This can cause friction if there is inadequate appreciation and integration of all contributions.

• Conflicting personal or departmental goals: Often, team members come from departments or functional areas with different priorities. Without clear alignment of goals, tensions may arise.

11.5.2. Promoting Open and Honest Communication

One of the most effective strategies for managing conflicts in diverse teams is to promote open and honest communication. Creating an environment where team members feel free to express their concerns or ideas without fear of retaliation is crucial for resolving conflicts constructively.

Strategies:

• Facilitating transparent dialogue: Encourage open and regular discussions where team members can address any disagreements directly and constructively. Tools such as retrospectives or meetings dedicated to conflict resolution can be useful for this purpose.

• Continuous feedback: Implement a continuous feedback system that allows team members to communicate promptly when issues arise. Timely feedback can prevent escalation of conflicts.

11.5.3. Using Conflict as an Opportunity for Growth

Conflict should not be viewed solely as an obstacle but as an opportunity to improve team dynamics and strengthen collaboration. Addressing conflicts with the intention to learn from each other and improve internal processes can lead to more effective solutions.

Strategies:

• Solution-oriented approach: Rather than focusing on who is right or wrong, guide the team toward finding practical solutions that satisfy all stakeholders. This approach strengthens group cohesion and encourages members to work together toward a common goal.

• Promoting empathy and mutual understanding: Encourage team members to put themselves in each other's shoes to better understand their perspectives and needs. This can reduce tension levels and lead to quicker and more harmonious conflict resolutions.

11.5.4. Facilitating Mediation and Support

In some cases, conflicts may require the intervention of an external facilitator or a leader to act as a mediator. The role of the facilitator is to help the parties involved find common ground and work together to resolve disagreements.

Strategies:

• Role of the leader as a facilitator: The team leader, or a designated facilitator, should step in when conflicts cannot be resolved internally. Their task is to ensure that discussions remain constructive and focused on problem resolution.

• Neutral mediation: In more complex cases, it may be helpful to involve a neutral third party to mediate the conflict. This external figure can provide an impartial perspective and help manage particularly delicate situations.

11.5.5. Developing Conflict Resolution Skills

An essential aspect of preventing and managing conflicts is developing conflict resolution skills within the team. Providing members with the tools and resources to address disagreements effectively can prevent escalation of issues and foster a more harmonious work environment.

Strategies:

• Training on soft skills: Offer training programs that include the development of communication, empathy, and conflict resolution skills. This helps create a team capable of independently managing internal tensions.

• Work on cultural awareness: In international or intercultural teams, it is important to raise team members' awareness of the cultural differences that can influence behaviors and expectations. A more informed approach will help prevent misunderstandings.

11.5.6. Creating a Culture of Respect and Inclusion

Finally, effective conflict management depends on creating a culture of mutual respect and inclusion, where differences are celebrated and not seen as obstacles.

Strategies:

- Promoting mutual respect: Implement policies and practices that ensure respect for all voices within the team. This can be reinforced through team-building initiatives and workshops on inclusivity.
- Celebrating diversity: Go beyond simple tolerance of differences by promoting an attitude that celebrates diversity as a source of strength and innovation for the team.

Creating a work environment where conflicts are addressed constructively and transformed into opportunities for growth not only strengthens team bonds but also contributes to improved operational effectiveness and innovation.

Chapter 12

Performance Evaluation in Diverse Teams

Chapter 12 - Performance Evaluation in Diverse Teams

Performance evaluation is a fundamental element in any team management approach, and it becomes even more crucial in heterogeneous contexts where skills, backgrounds, and objectives can vary considerably. In this chapter, we analyze the importance of measuring team performance fairly and effectively, focusing on how to adapt such measurements to the needs of multidisciplinary groups with diverse objectives.

12.1. Equity in Performance Evaluation

When it comes to heterogeneous teams, composed of individuals with different skills and backgrounds, the concept of equity in performance evaluation becomes crucial. In such a varied environment, applying a standard and uniform approach risks penalizing some individuals while overvaluing others. Equity does not mean treating everyone the same way; rather, it means adapting the evaluation to account for differences in roles, responsibilities, and contributions, without overlooking the importance of collaboration and the overall contribution to the project.

12.1.1. Diversification of Evaluation Criteria

In a diverse team, the skills range from technical to more creative, including organizational or support roles. Applying identical evaluation parameters for all members does not reflect the reality of their functions. A software engineer might be evaluated based on the efficiency of their code, while a project manager should be assessed on their ability to coordinate the team and meet deadlines.

To ensure equity, it is necessary to develop a set of evaluation criteria specific to each role. This means recognizing the specificity of contributions: on one hand, the concrete results achieved individually, and on the other, the support provided to the group in reaching common goals. The criteria should therefore be customized while maintaining an underlying consistency to avoid obvious disparities.

12.1.2. Transparency in Evaluation Processes

Another essential element for ensuring equity is the transparency of evaluation processes. In heterogeneous teams, a lack of clarity regarding the criteria used can generate frustration, especially if some members feel they are being evaluated unfairly compared to their peers. Transparency not only fosters a climate of trust but also provides each member the opportunity to better understand how to improve their contributions.

For this reason, the evaluation criteria must be explicitly communicated and shared with the team. Each member should know which parameters are used to assess their performance, understand the importance of these parameters, and how they fit into the overall project context. Involving the team in defining the evaluation metrics can be an additional tool to achieve consensus and strengthen the culture of transparency.

12.1.3. Valuing Invisible Contributions

In a diverse team, some contributions are more visible and easily measurable than others. For example, it is often straightforward to quantify a software developer's performance in terms of code written or bugs resolved, but it is more difficult to measure the contribution of those who foster group cohesion, facilitate communication, or resolve interpersonal issues.

To make evaluation fairer, it is essential to recognize and value these "invisible" contributions as well. This can occur through the adoption of peer feedback tools or the inclusion of qualitative indicators, such as leadership ability, willingness to support colleagues, and conflict resolution skills. Having a comprehensive and balanced view of performance means considering the impact each individual has not only on tangible results but also on the well-being and productivity of the team as a whole.

12.1.4. Contribution to Collective Success

Finally, equity cannot overlook the analysis of each individual's contribution to the overall success of the team. In heterogeneous groups, the complementarity of skills is often the key to achieving ambitious objectives, and the value of each member must also be evaluated based on how their skills intertwine with those of others.

This implies alignment between individual evaluation and team performance: members must be incentivized to work for the common good, not just for individual performance. The integration of personal results and their overall impact on the team represents a fair and holistic approach to performance evaluation.

In summary, equity in performance evaluation within heterogeneous teams requires a tailored approach that values diversity and enhances its potential. Only through flexible criteria, transparency, and attention to collective contributions can we ensure that all team members feel appreciated and motivated.

12.2. Measuring Performance in Diverse Teams

Evaluating performance in diverse teams requires a methodical and flexible approach that takes into account the different skills, roles, and responsibilities present within the group. While some members may contribute in an evident and measurable way, others add value through soft skills or with less tangible impacts. For this reason, it is crucial to develop a performance measurement system that reflects the complexity of teamwork without neglecting individual contributions.

12.2.1. Balancing Quantitative and Qualitative Metrics

In heterogeneous teams, performance cannot be evaluated solely through quantitative metrics, such as the amount of work completed or execution speed. Although these indicators are important, they do not represent the entire spectrum of individual or collective contributions.

To balance the analysis, it is essential to include qualitative metrics that measure less tangible elements, such as impact on team culture, problem-solving abilities, quality of collaboration, and creativity in finding innovative solutions. These dimensions, often invisible in numerical data, can have a decisive influence on the success of the project. Carefully measuring these competencies allows for highlighting the contributions of those who may not excel in standard metrics but still play a crucial role.

12.2.2. Customizing Performance Objectives

Another essential aspect is the customization of performance objectives. In a diverse team, each member has unique skills and strengths that must be considered when defining performance goals. Setting equal objectives for all members risks penalizing those with more complex or non-operational roles.

The ideal approach is to build tailored objectives for each team member, in line with their skills and role. For example, a software developer might be evaluated based on the quality of their code and the effectiveness of the proposed solutions, while a team coordinator could have objectives related to time management, communication, and support provided to other members. Customizing objectives creates a context of equity, where everyone is judged based on their specific contribution to the success of the project.

12.2.3. The Importance of Continuous Feedback

In dynamic and diverse contexts, performance measurement should not be limited to the end of the project or formal evaluation meetings. Continuous feedback is a fundamental component to ensure that team members understand their progress and can adapt their contributions in real time.

Regular feedback allows for quickly resolving any difficulties, reducing friction between team members, and promoting constant improvements. In this context, it is useful to adopt a 360-degree feedback model, where individual performance is evaluated not only by supervisors but also by peers, external collaborators, and other stakeholders. This way, a more comprehensive and nuanced view of performance is obtained.

12.2.4. Integrating Team Success and Individual Contribution

Finally, it is essential that the performance measurement system reflects both the success of the team as a whole and individual contributions. In a heterogeneous work environment, the performance of each individual is closely intertwined with that of others. Measuring the effectiveness of the group as a unit allows for recognizing the value of collaboration and teamwork, integrating personal results with collective ones.

A good measurement system should therefore evaluate how each individual contributes to achieving common objectives, valuing behaviors that promote cohesion and collective success. By doing so, a sense of belonging and responsibility is fostered, motivating members to work not only for their personal success but also for that of the team.

In summary, measuring performance in diverse teams requires a combination of quantitative and qualitative metrics, customized objectives, and a strong focus on continuous feedback and collaboration. This approach ensures that every contribution is assessed fairly and that all team members feel valued for their input to the common success.

12.3. Adapting Assessments to Team Diversity

In a team composed of individuals with different skills, experiences, and backgrounds, performance evaluation methods must be appropriately adapted to reflect this complexity. The diversity of approaches, work styles, and knowledge can pose a challenge for a traditional evaluation system, which often does not take these variables into account. For this reason, it is essential to develop a system that respects and values differences, allowing each team member to be assessed fairly and pertinently.

12.3.1. Recognizing Cultural and Professional Differences

A heterogeneous team may include individuals from different cultural backgrounds, with work approaches that can vary significantly. Some members may place more importance on collaboration and communication, while others may focus more on efficiency and results. Evaluating performance without considering these differences risks penalizing those who adopt a style different from the dominant paradigm.

An effective evaluation system must therefore be able to recognize these differences, preventing a person's culture or work style from negatively influencing the assessment of their performance. This requires an open and flexible mindset from leaders, who must be able to appreciate diversity as a resource rather than viewing it as an obstacle.

12.3.2. Customizing Evaluation Criteria

To adapt performance evaluations to a heterogeneous team, it is helpful to customize criteria based on the specific skills and responsibilities of each member. Standardized criteria, which do not take into account differences in roles and competencies, may be ineffective or unfair in this context.

For example, a team member who handles customer management may be evaluated based on their ability to manage relationships and solve problems, while a technician specialized in a field such as cybersecurity might be judged based on their ability to implement complex technical solutions. Defining specific criteria for each role allows for better recognition of each individual's unique skills and provides a more accurate picture of their performance.

12.3.3. Creating Spaces for Individual Feedback

In a diverse team, open and continuous communication is crucial for understanding how each member perceives their contribution and identifying any difficulties related to the group's diversity. Creating specific moments for individual feedback allows team members to express their concerns or suggest improvements to work processes.

This feedback should not be one-sided: leaders must also be ready to receive suggestions from team members on how to improve diversity management and how to further adapt evaluation criteria. A constant and open dialogue on these issues helps create an inclusive work environment where each individual feels valued and respected.

12.3.4. Fostering a Continuous Learning Environment

Finally, it is important that performance evaluations in diverse teams do not just measure final results but also encourage continuous learning. The diversity within the team represents a great opportunity for mutual growth, as group members can learn from each other, discovering new approaches and perspectives.

An effective evaluation system should therefore reward not only the achievement of goals but also the commitment to learning and adapting to new contexts or skills. This encourages a corporate culture based on growth, where diversity is seen as a resource for innovation and continuous improvement.

In summary, adapting evaluations to team diversity requires flexibility, customization of evaluation criteria, spaces for individual feedback, and the promotion of a continuous learning environment. This approach ensures that every team member is assessed fairly, in line with their skills and specific contributions.

12.4. Monitoring and Adapting Evaluation Parameters

Effective performance evaluation requires that the parameters used to monitor the team's progress be continuously reviewed and adapted. In a dynamic context like that of heterogeneous teams, the parameters initially established may not always be relevant or sufficient to reflect the actual contributions of the members. For this reason, it is essential that leaders adopt a flexible approach and periodically review evaluation criteria to ensure they align with the team's objectives and the evolution of roles.

12.4.1. Defining Realistic and Customized Objectives

When monitoring the performance of a diverse team, it is crucial that the goals set are realistic and take into account the specifics of each individual. Team members with advanced technical skills may require less time to achieve certain milestones, while those who are still adapting or working in areas new to them may need more support and time.

An approach that involves assigning customized objectives allows for a more accurate assessment of each member's performance. Leaders should therefore establish goals that are motivating and challenging but also achievable, taking into account the context and specific skills.

12.4.2. Measuring Short- and Long-Term Performance

A balanced evaluation system should not focus solely on immediate results but also consider long-term performance. This is particularly important in heterogeneous teams, where the evolution of skills can vary. Some members may show rapid improvements on short-term projects, while others may excel on more complex, long-term projects, where continuous learning and skill maturation play a crucial role.

Performance metrics must thus be balanced to capture not only short-term successes but also the ability to adapt, grow, and contribute sustainably in the long term. This allows for a more comprehensive and fair assessment of the value each team member brings.

12.4.3. Periodically Reviewing Evaluation Parameters

Given the constantly evolving nature of heterogeneous teams, evaluation parameters must be regularly reviewed to adapt to organizational changes, new strategic objectives, or modifications within the team. For example, a team may initially be evaluated based on operational efficiency, but over time, with the growth of the team and increasing project complexity, it may be necessary to introduce parameters that consider innovation, problem-solving, or collaboration capabilities.

This periodic review ensures that evaluation criteria remain relevant and capable of measuring fundamental aspects of the team's contribution, avoiding the use of obsolete metrics that no longer reflect the needs of the project or organization.

12.4.4. Balancing Individual and Group Performance

In the context of heterogeneous teams, it is crucial to find a balance between evaluating individual performance and that of the group. While each team member has specific objectives and responsibilities, it is equally important to assess the contribution each makes to collective success. Teams with diverse backgrounds can generate unique synergies, and often the value an individual brings is not limited to their work but also affects the overall effectiveness of the group.

A good evaluation system should therefore consider not only individual results but also the impact that each member's work has on the cohesion and overall outcomes of the team. This helps to promote a culture of collaboration, recognizing the value of individual skills within the broader context of the group.

In summary, monitoring and adapting evaluation parameters in a diverse team requires flexibility, attention to individual and collective objectives, and a constant review of criteria to ensure they reflect the team's and projects' evolution. This approach ensures that performance is measured fairly and pertinently, fostering both personal growth and the overall success of the group.

SECTION 4: Beyond the Methodology

Chapter 13

The Holistic Approach in IT: A Paradigm for Diverse Teams and Complex Projects

Chapter 13 - The Holistic Approach in IT: A Paradigm for Diverse Teams and Complex Projects

Chapter 13 - The Holistic Approach in IT: A Paradigm for Diverse Teams and Complex Projects

13.1. Definition and Principles of the Holistic Approach in Business Agility

In the context of Agile Synergy, a holistic approach is not just an operational strategy but a necessity for managing the complexities of diverse teams and modern business ecosystems. Unlike a traditional approach that fragments the system into isolated components, holism is based on the understanding that every part of an organization is interconnected. This means that technological decisions, team dynamics, and decision-making processes are deeply intertwined with human, cultural, and market factors.

13.1.1. Fundamental Elements of the Holistic Approach

• Interconnectivity: Every team, technology, and decision is linked to a broader network, where changes in one area can have consequences in others. The holistic approach recognizes this complexity and promotes systemic thinking.

• Multilevel Integration: Instead of working in silos, teams and processes are integrated to promote synergies among technical, organizational, and human competencies.

• Balance between Technology and People: Managing technologies must go hand in hand with understanding human and cultural needs. Usability, corporate culture, and user experience become central.

• Long-Term Perspective: Decisions are not merely focused on solving immediate problems but are evaluated for their long-term impact on the entire business ecosystem.

13.1.2. Benefits of a Holistic Approach

• Effective Complexity Management: This approach allows for clearer navigation through the increasing complexity in an evolving business environment, recognizing the interdependence of technical and human variables.

• Interdisciplinary Collaboration: It fosters a culture of collaboration among diverse competencies within the team, creating more innovative and balanced solutions.

• Adaptability and Resilience: It helps teams respond more quickly and efficiently to changes or challenges, adapting more easily to new market and technological dynamics.

• Efficiency and Continuous Innovation: An integrated approach stimulates innovative solutions that emerge from the interaction between different levels of competencies, enhancing operational efficiency.

13.1.3. Application of the Holistic Approach in Agile Synergy

In the context of Agile Synergy, the holistic approach proves particularly useful in situations where technological complexity and human needs intertwine. From managing large IT infrastructures to developing large-scale software, and managing high-uncertainty projects, holism offers guidance for making more informed and sustainable decisions.

13.2. Benefits of the Holistic Approach

Adopting a holistic approach within the context of Agile Synergy brings advantages that extend beyond simple project management. This approach can radically transform work dynamics within teams and play a crucial role in modern IT environments. Let's explore how:

13.2.1. Advanced Complexity Management

In the IT world, characterized by increasingly complex systems, technological and human elements constantly interact. The holistic approach allows for the consideration of these interactions as a whole, rather than focusing on individual components. This enables more effective complexity management, reducing the risk of errors and misunderstandings while improving the overall quality of solutions.

13.2.2. Promotion of Interdisciplinary Collaboration

In diverse IT teams, competencies range from data analysis to cybersecurity, from frontend to backend development. The holistic approach facilitates the integration of these skills, creating a cohesive unit and a collaborative environment where each member can contribute significantly with their expertise. This enriches the final product and enhances the experience of every team member.

13.2.3. Adaptability to Change and Volatility

In a context where technology and the market evolve rapidly, the holistic approach fosters the flexibility necessary to respond promptly to changes. Rigidity gives way to dynamic adaptability, allowing teams to effectively tackle challenges and seize opportunities, even in unpredictable settings.

13.2.4. Resource Optimization and Increased Efficiency

A holistic approach ensures the efficient use of resources, avoiding overlaps and redundancies. This leads to cost reductions and greater operational efficiency, ensuring that every resource is utilized harmoniously and integrated with the rest of the system.

13.2.5. Focus on User Experience and Customer Satisfaction

Considering the entire ecosystem of a project, including end users, leads to more integrated and well-designed solutions. This approach not only meets technical requirements but also optimizes the user experience, positively impacting customer satisfaction.

13.2.6. Proactive Problem Prevention and Risk Reduction

Thanks to the comprehensive view characteristic of the holistic approach, teams can anticipate problems before they arise. This allows for the identification of potential risks arising from interactions between various components of the system, reducing the likelihood of isolated or uncoordinated solutions.

Chapter 13 - The Holistic Approach in IT: A Paradigm for Diverse Teams and Complex Projects

In summary, the holistic approach in Agile Synergy is not just a strategy for managing complex projects but represents a true work philosophy. By promoting collaboration, adaptability, and a global perspective, this approach becomes essential for success in today's technological environment, characterized by rapid evolution and increasingly deep interconnections.

13.3. Conclusion: Embracing Holism in the Digital Age

In the rapidly evolving technological landscape, adopting a holistic approach in IT is no longer just a choice but a strategic necessity. With the increasing complexity of IT systems and their growing integration into every aspect of modern life, holism becomes a crucial tool for addressing the challenges of technological innovation and successfully navigating this changing context.

13.3.1. Recognizing Interdependence

The holistic approach highlights the importance of recognizing and respecting the interdependence among different components of IT systems. Every technical decision not only affects the functionality of a single element but also has broader consequences, such as team cohesion, customer experience, and business strategy. Only an integrated view can lead to informed and sustainable decisions.

13.3.2. Responding to Contemporary Challenges

Modern challenges, such as cybersecurity, scalability, and the need for constant innovation, require a deep understanding of both technological and human dynamics. The holistic approach provides a perspective that goes beyond pure technology, allowing for a balance between these complex needs and a strategic, sustainable vision.

13.3.3. Fostering a Culture of Collaboration and Innovation

Adopting a holistic vision promotes a corporate culture that centers on collaboration and continuous innovation. Multidisciplinary teams can join forces and experiment with new solutions that transcend traditional boundaries, creating a more inclusive and creative work environment.

13.3.4. Preparing for the Future

The holistic approach prepares organizations and IT professionals for a future in which complexity and interconnection will increase exponentially. With a comprehensive view, the tools and capabilities necessary to tackle rapid changes are developed, ensuring adaptability and foresight in a constantly evolving world.

In conclusion, the holistic approach in IT is not merely an operational method but a work philosophy that embraces change and values the connections between technology and humanity. With this integrated vision, IT professionals can navigate confidently and successfully through the complex and fascinating modern technological landscape.

Chapter 13 - The Holistic Approach in IT: A Paradigm for Diverse Teams and Complex Projects

Chapter 13 - The Holistic Approach in IT: A Paradigm for Diverse Teams and Complex Projects

Chapter 14

Proactive Change Management: Anticipating and Adapting in the Agile Era

Chapter 14 - Proactive Change Management: Anticipating and Adapting in the Agile Era

Chapter 14 - Proactive Change Management: Anticipating and Adapting in the Agile Era

This chapter delves into the heart of "Proactive Change Management," a fundamental skill in the dynamic world of agile development. In a context where change is the only constant, the ability to manage these changes proactively is not just useful but essential for the success of any project.

14.1. Managing Pauses and Resuming Projects

Within the Agile Synergy framework, managing pauses and resuming projects is crucial for ensuring the continuity and success of long-term initiatives. Pauses, or temporary "hibernations," may be necessary for various reasons, including strategic realignment, changes in business priorities, or unforeseen external factors. Similarly, resuming projects requires careful planning to restart without compromising the quality or cohesion of the work done thus far.

14.1.1. Clear Decision and Communication

Before suspending a project, it is essential to conduct a thorough analysis of the impact that such a pause will have on resources, the team, and the overall project goals. This decision must be communicated clearly to all stakeholders involved, with an emphasis on:

- The reasons for the suspension: Providing transparent motivations to team members helps prevent misunderstandings or uncertainties.
- The expectations for resumption: Indicating, if possible, a rough timeline for resumption, even if subject to change, helps keep everyone aligned.

14.1.2. Documenting the Current State

Before pausing a project, it is vital to document the current state in detail, ensuring that all progress, outcomes, and open issues are clearly recorded. This includes:

- Achieved progress: Each completed milestone should be clearly identified and archived.
- Pending tasks: Incomplete tasks must be tracked so that the project can be resumed without loss of information.

14.1.3. Resuming the Project

When deciding to resume a project, it is crucial to evaluate the internal and external conditions that led to the suspension. Before restarting work, it is necessary to:

- Review the previous state: Reexamine the documentation prepared during the suspension to get updated on progress and any open issues.
- Update the project plan: Adapt the initial plan to reflect changes in context and business priorities, ensuring that everyone is aligned with the current objectives.

Chapter 14 - Proactive Change Management: Anticipating and Adapting in the Agile Era

14.1.4. Resource Reallocation and Monitoring

Resuming a project often requires reallocating both human and technical resources to adapt to new needs and revised priorities. It is important to:

• Assign adequate resources: Ensure that the right personnel and technologies are available for the resumption of the project.
• Monitor progress: Use monitoring tools to ensure that the project resumes smoothly, allowing for quick adjustments in case of issues.

In this way, Agile Synergy enables proactive management of project pauses and resumptions, ensuring that every interruption is approached strategically and with minimal impact on operational continuity.

14.2. Adaptive Planning Model

In the context of Agile Synergy, the ability to adapt planning is essential for keeping the project flexible and responsive to changes. Adaptive planning allows projects to be divided into more manageable modules, each with clear objectives and priorities, enabling real-time adjustments without compromising the overall vision of the project.

14.2.1. Project Modularity

One of the key principles of adaptive planning is modularity. Instead of managing projects as monoliths, Agile Synergy suggests breaking each initiative into smaller, independent parts:

- **Module Definition**: Each module should have clear objectives and defined outcomes, making it autonomous from others while still integrated into the whole.
- **Ease of Management**: Modularity allows for modifying, moving, or eliminating individual components without significantly impacting the entire project.

14.2.2. Iterative Planning and Short Cycles

Iterative planning is another central pillar of Agile Synergy. Short planning cycles ensure the ability to quickly adapt to new information or changes in priorities:

- **Short and Dynamic Cycles**: For example, bi-weekly or monthly planning allows for frequent reviews of project status and timely modifications.
- **Continuous Review**: In each cycle, the team analyzes the progress made, identifies any obstacles, and adjusts priorities for the next cycle.

14.2.3. Flexibility of the Module

In addition to division into modules, it is crucial that each module be flexible and modifiable during execution:

- **Checkpoints:** Implementing regular checkpoints to evaluate the status of each module helps identify any needs for revision or adjustment.
- **Immediate Adaptation:** In the event of changes in business priorities or customer requirements, modules can be easily added, moved, or modified without having to redo the entire project plan.

In summary, adaptive planning and modularity allow for proactive and flexible project management, enabling rapid responses to challenges and the ability to seize emerging opportunities. Agile Synergy thus provides an agile framework that simplifies managing complexity in a dynamic environment.

14.3. Risk Management Toold and Contingency Planning

Within the framework of Agile Synergy, the proactive identification and management of risk are essential for ensuring the long-term success of projects. The ability to respond quickly to uncertainties and to have robust contingency plans enables teams to maintain control even in times of crisis or sudden change.

14.3.1. Proactive Risk Analysis

A holistic approach requires a continuous assessment of potential risks that may emerge along the way:

• Continuous Monitoring: Risk analysis should be an ongoing process, utilizing advanced tools such as SWOT analysis or root cause analysis to anticipate and prevent issues before they arise.

• Team Collaboration: Each team member, with their specific expertise, contributes to identifying and assessing risks, ensuring a comprehensive view of potential vulnerabilities.

14.3.2. Development of Contingency Plans

Anticipating future scenarios and planning appropriate responses is crucial for maintaining project agility:

• Scenario Planning: Developing contingency plans based on various scenarios allows teams to prepare for a wide range of possibilities, minimizing risks associated with unforeseen situations.

• Flexibility and Adaptability: Contingency plans should be dynamic, allowing for rapid adjustments based on evolving circumstances. This ensures a prompt and effective response to any change or crisis.

14.3.3. Implementation of Risk Management Tools

Utilizing digital tools is essential for dynamically monitoring risks and planning responses:

Chapter 14 - Proactive Change Management: Anticipating and Adapting in the Agile Era

• Interactive Dashboards: Tools like JIRA or ServiceNow can be used to track risks in real-time, providing a clear overview of potential issues and the solutions to be implemented.

• Alerts and Notifications: Setting up alerts to signal emerging problems or significant deviations from the project plan allows the team to act promptly, preventing negative impacts.

14.3.4. Culture of Proactivity and Preparedness

Finally, fostering a corporate culture that values proactivity and preparedness is vital:

• Training and Awareness: Providing regular training to the team on risk management tools and practices ensures that everyone is ready to respond to changes.

• Simulations and Testing: Conducting simulations and tests of contingency plans helps prepare the team and ensures that responses are smooth and timely when needed.

CONCLUSION

Chapter 15

Towards an Agile Future: Maturity, Limits, and Next Horizons

Chapter 15 - Towards an Agile Future: Maturity, Limits, and Next Horizons

Chapter 15 - Towards an Agile Future: Maturity, Limits, and Next Horizons

15.1. Holism as a Foundation for Innovation and Resilience

Holism is a concept that originates from the Greek word "ὄλος" (hòlos), which means "total" or "global." This theoretical position asserts that the properties of a system cannot be fully explained through its individual components, as the whole is always greater or different from the sum of its parts. In contrast to the reductionist approach, which analyzes systems by breaking them down into their basic elements, holism considers the whole in a broader and more integrated context.

The holistic approach we have explored throughout this book offers a solid foundation for stimulating innovation and resilience within organizations, especially in complex contexts like IT and industrial environments. As we have seen, holism does not limit itself to considering individual elements separately but addresses the business reality as a set of interconnected parts that work in synergy. This systemic vision enables teams to overcome barriers between departments, promoting a culture of collaboration and continuous improvement.

15.1.1. Interconnection as a Key Success Factor

The interconnection between teams, technologies, and processes is fundamental for addressing modern challenges.

In a constantly evolving world, where technological change is rapid and customer needs frequently change, being able to integrate all aspects of a project becomes essential. It is not just a matter of tools and processes, but also of mindset. Companies that adopt a holistic approach can anticipate changes and adapt more quickly because they have a comprehensive view that allows them to recognize in advance the interactions between different variables.

15.1.2. Holism as a Driver of Innovation

Innovation, one of the pillars of Agile Synergy, develops more easily in a holistic environment. When people do not work in silos but understand the interconnection between various aspects of the business, innovative ideas flourish. This approach allows teams to see problems from different perspectives, thereby contributing to creative and original solutions. Innovation is not just technical, but also organizational: the integration between business strategies and operational teams allows for continuous and sustainable transformation.

15.1.3. Resilience Through a Global Perspective

Business resilience is another key outcome of a holistic approach. Resilient organizations not only manage to withstand changes but know how to adapt quickly and even take advantage of adversity. In a holistic context, every decision considers the long-term consequences and the interconnections between various business elements. This means that companies are capable of absorbing shocks and reorganizing in a short time, without compromising their operations or the quality of their products and services.

Ultimately, holism represents an indispensable foundation for building an organization capable of constant innovation and successfully facing future challenges. This mindset must be rooted at every level of the company, from leadership to operational teams, thus creating a favorable environment for the development of effective, creative, and resilient solutions.

15.2. Integrating the Organizational Dimension and Global Strategy

The ability to integrate the organizational dimension with the global strategy represents one of the greatest achievements of organizations adopting a holistic approach. In the context of Agile Synergy, this integration becomes essential to align the strategic vision with operational execution, ensuring that every team, process, and technology is aligned with long-term business objectives.

15.2.1. Alignment Between Strategic Vision and Operational Practices

In many organizations, global strategy and operational practices are managed separately, creating a disconnection between what the company wants to achieve and how daily activities are executed. Agile Synergy seeks to eliminate this division, fostering a natural integration between strategic vision and operational activities. This means that strategic decisions must always be translated into concrete objectives for teams and that operational practices must always be reviewed in light of the long-term strategy.

The holistic approach ensures that every action is consistent with the organization's overall vision, allowing for proactive resource management and rapid responses to emerging challenges. Operational teams, within this context, are not merely executors but actively contribute to achieving the strategic vision, enhancing the feedback and innovation cycle.

15.2.2. Coordination Among Hierarchical and Functional Levels

The integration between the organizational dimension and the global strategy also requires strong coordination among the various hierarchical and functional levels of the company. It is not just a matter of well-defined processes but also of corporate culture. The holistic approach promotes active collaboration between executives and operational teams, creating a work environment where feedback from the bottom influences strategic decisions, and directives from the top effectively guide daily activities.

Holism pushes companies to transcend traditional boundaries between departments and teams, making cross-functional collaboration a priority. This alignment between organizational levels helps avoid disconnections and misunderstandings, facilitating a continuous and transparent flow of information. Executives can make better decisions thanks to direct feedback from field teams, while teams have a clear view of business priorities and long-term strategies.

15.2.3. Adapting Strategy Based on Context Evolution

The integration of the organizational dimension and the global strategy cannot be static. Modern organizations operate in rapidly changing contexts, meaning that business strategy must evolve alongside shifting market and technology conditions. The holistic approach allows for greater adaptability, enabling organizations to change their direction without disorienting operational teams.

Through Agile Synergy, companies can quickly adjust their strategic objectives in response to new challenges or opportunities. Regular reviews of operational practices and strategy ensure that the company remains competitive and resilient, capable of facing any change. Teams, in turn, are encouraged to maintain a flexible mindset, ready to reorganize their activities based on new business priorities.

In conclusion, the integration of the organizational dimension with the global strategy is the cornerstone of effective business management within Agile Synergy. This enables the creation of an organization that not only responds rapidly to changes but can anticipate them, remaining aligned with long-term objectives while addressing present challenges.

15.3. Preparing for the Future: The Evolution of Agility and Its Limits

As highlighted in the journey of Agile Synergy, agility represents a powerful tool for managing projects and business processes, but it is essential to recognize that this approach, no matter how flexible, has its limits. While the Agile model has proven to be a valuable resource for adapting to rapid changes and fostering collaboration, it is increasingly approaching a stage of maturity where its structural limits begin to emerge. This final segment of the chapter explores future prospects and sets the stage for in-depth discussion in the next book.

15.3.1. Maturity of Agility

Agility, while demonstrating its effectiveness across various sectors, begins to reveal its limitations when implemented in more complex or large-scale contexts. Many teams find that as projects grow, managing change and coordinating among numerous groups requires an evolution of the framework itself. The standardization of processes, while maintaining flexibility, becomes a significant challenge. This is where the natural limits of the Agile approach emerge: the difficulty in managing large-scale operations and the need to find a balance between agility and stability.

Chapter 15 - Towards an Agile Future: Maturity, Limits, and Next Horizons

15.3.2. Beyond Agility: The Future of Business Management

The holistic approach becomes essential when organizations face challenges of growth and internationalization. As discussed in this chapter, integrating the organizational dimension with global strategy provides a solid foundation for addressing increasingly complex contexts. However, the question remains: is agility, as we know it, sufficient to guide organizations in the long term? In the next book, we will explore how agility, originally conceived as an innovative tool, might transform to address the limits it is beginning to reach.

As the business world continues to evolve, it is crucial to explore how agile management can integrate with other methodologies and emerging new models of leadership. This means looking beyond the current principles of agility to embrace a broader and more strategic vision.

15.3.3. Innovation and Change: Preparing for the Next Phase

Finally, preparing for the future is not just about technological innovation or process improvement, but a radical rethink of how we manage change and adaptation. Agility, as a concept, may be nearing a new evolution, driven by the limits we have explored. The next book will focus on this transition, examining how companies can integrate complex organizational dimensions and global strategies, pushing agility beyond its current boundaries.

In conclusion, this chapter does not mark the end of the journey, but the beginning of a new reflection on the evolution of agility. The foundations laid by the Agile Synergy Methodology represent a starting point for

Chapter 15 - Towards an Agile Future: Maturity, Limits, and Next Horizons

exploring the new paths that lie ahead. In the next book, we will delve deeper into the themes of this transition, reflecting on how to tackle the challenges of the future and how to integrate the organizational dimension and global strategy to build truly sustainable agility.

References

Appendix - References

References

"Agile Project Management with Scrum" di Ken Schwaber

"Lean Software Development: An Agile Toolkit" di Mary Poppendieck e Tom Poppendieck

"User Stories Applied: For Agile Software Development" di Mike Cohn

"Succeeding with Agile: Software Development Using Scrum" di Mike Cohn

"Kanban: Successful Evolutionary Change for Your Technology Business" di David J. Anderson

"Agile Estimating and Planning" di Mike Cohn

"The Phoenix Project: A Novel About IT, DevOps, and Helping Your Business Win" di Gene Kim, Kevin Behr, e George Spafford

"Continuous Delivery: Reliable Software Releases through Build, Test, and Deployment Automation" di Jez Humble e David Farley

"Extreme Programming Explained: Embrace Change" di Kent Beck"The Lean Startup: How Today's Entrepreneurs Use Continuous Innovation to Create Radically Successful Businesses" di Eric Ries

"Scrum: The Art of Doing Twice the Work in Half the Time" di Jeff Sutherland

"Agile Testing: A Practical Guide for Testers and Agile Teams" di Lisa Crispin e Janet Gregory

"Implementing Lean Software Development: From Concept to Cash" di Mary e Tom Poppendieck

"The Art of Agile Development" di James Shore

"Coaching Agile Teams: A Companion for ScrumMasters, Agile Coaches, and Project Managers in Transition" di Lyssa Adkins

"The Agile Samurai: How Agile Masters Deliver Great Software" di Jonathan Rasmusson

"The Principles of Product Development Flow: Second Generation Lean Product Development" di Donald G. Reinertsen

"Crystal Clear: A Human-Powered Methodology for Small Teams" di Alistair Cockburn

"Managing Agile Projects" di Sanjiv Augustine

"Agile Retrospectives: Making Good Teams Great" di Esther Derby e Diana Larsen

"Agile Product Management with Scrum: Creating Products that Customers Love" di Roman Pichler

"Essential Scrum: A Practical Guide to the Most Popular Agile Process" di Kenneth S. Rubin

"Agile Software Development: The Cooperative Game" di Alistair Cockburn

"Project Management Institute: A Guide to the Project Management Body of Knowledge (PMBOK Guide)"

"A study of the Scrum Master's role" - J. Noll, M. A. Razzak, J. M. Bass, S. Beecham

"The rise and evolution of Agile Software Development" - R. Hoda, N. Salleh, J. Grundy

"Developing high-performing teams: a design thinking led approach" - H. Keighran, S. Adikari

"Cross-Functional Team in a project with an Agile management: effective strategies and common challenges in a cross-functional team while using agile project management" - A. Zegarra, S. Saban

"Olismo" https://it.wikipedia.org/wiki/Olismo

Appendix - References

www.ingramcontent.com/pod-product-compliance
Lightning Source LLC
Chambersburg PA
CBHW052141220526

45471CB00004B/1477